LIVES OF GREAT RELIGIOUS BOOKS

Thomas Aquinas's *Summa theologiae*

LIVES OF GREAT RELIGIOUS BOOKS

Thomas Aquinas's *Summa theologiae*, Bernard McGinn
The *Dead Sea Scrolls*, John J. Collins
The *Bhagavad Gita*, Richard H. Davis
The *Book of Mormon*, Paul C. Gutjahr
The Book of *Genesis*, Ronald Hendel
The *Book of Common Prayer*, Alan Jacobs
The Book of *Job*, Mark Larrimore
The Tibetan Book of the Dead, Donald S. Lopez, Jr.
Dietrich Bonhoeffer's *Letters and Papers from Prison*, Martin E. Marty
The *I Ching*, Richard J. Smith
The *Yoga Sutras of Patanjali*, David Gordon White
Augustine's *Confessions*, Garry Wills

FORTHCOMING:

The Book of *Revelation*, Timothy Beal
Confucius's *Analects*, Annping Chin and Jonathan D. Spence
Josephus's *Jewish War*, Martin Goodman
John Calvin's *Institutes of the Christian Religion*, Bruce Gordon
The *Lotus Sutra*, Donald S. Lopez, Jr.
C. S. Lewis's *Mere Christianity*, George Marsden
The Greatest Translations of All Time: The *Septuagint* and the
    Vulgate, Jack Miles
The Passover *Haggadah*, Vanessa Ochs
The Song of Songs, Ilana Pardes
The *Daode Jing*, James Robson
Rumi's *Masnavi*, Omid Safi
The *Talmud*, Barry Wimpfheimer

Thomas Aquinas's
Summa theologiae

A BIOGRAPHY

Bernard McGinn

PRINCETON UNIVERSITY PRESS

Princeton and Oxford

To my classmates at the North American College

Class of 1963

Ad multos annos, gloriosque annos, vivas!

CONTENTS

PREFACE   ix

INTRODUCTION   1

CHAPTER 1
The World That Made Thomas Aquinas   7

CHAPTER 2
Creating the *Summa theologiae*   19

CHAPTER 3
A Tour of the *Summa theologiae*   74

CHAPTER 4
The Tides of Thomism, 1275–1850   117

CHAPTER 5
The Rise and Fall of Neothomism   163

EPILOGUE   210

ABBREVIATIONS FOR THOMAS'S WORKS 215

NOTES 217

BIBLIOGRAPHY 245
   Translations of the *Summa theologiae* 245
   General Books on Thomas and His
      Thought 246
   Particular Studies of Thomas's Thought
      Relating to the *Summa* 247
   Histories of Thomism 247
   Online Resources 248

INDEXES
   Name and Title Index 249
   Subject Index 254

This book owes its origin to the polite persistence of Fred Appel of Princeton University Press, who kept asking me to think of contributing something to a new series, Lives of Great Religious Books. I considered composing a short book on a mystical classic, such as Bernard of Clairvaux's *Sermons on the Song of Songs*, but the more I thought about the possibilities the more I was drawn to the scary idea of writing a book on Thomas Aquinas's *Summa theologiae*, one of the longest works in the canon of religious classics and one of the most studied. I am not a card-carrying member of any Thomist party and I've written only a few things on Thomas over my academic career. Nevertheless, I've been reading Thomas for almost sixty years and teaching him for over forty. When I was studying a dry-as-dust version of Neo-thomist philosophy from 1957 to 1959, I was rescued from despair by reading the works of Etienne Gilson, especially his *Being and Some Philosophers*. Doing theology at the Gregorian University in Rome between 1959 and 1963, I was privileged to work with two great modern investigators of Thomas, Joseph de Finance and Bernard Lonergan. It was then I realized that no matter what kind of theology one elects to pursue in life, there is no getting away from Thomas. So the opportunity to come back to Thomas and the *Summa* was both a challenge and a delight. Rereading the *Summa* and trying to catch up on at least some of the always-increasing literature on Aquinas was a homecoming. I hope the reader may be able to experience some of the intellectual stimulation I felt in what follows. I want to thank Fred Appel for valuable suggestions about shortening an originally bloated text to more manageable dimensions, and I also thank my wife, Patricia, for her customary discernment in helping with the editing process. Debbie Tegarden of Princeton University Press was unfailingly helpful in the editing process. My friends and colleagues Susan Schreiner and David Tracy gave valuable assistance with the last two chapters. Finally, three anonymous readers were also very helpful with corrections and suggestions. Any errors that remain are my own.

A Note on Citing Thomas

There is no best edition for all of Thomas Aquinas, although the Leonine Edition begun in 1880 and still under way offers a critical text for most of his writings, but not the *Summa theologiae*. I cite and translate the *Summa* from the student edition based on the Leonine text and published by the Biblioteca de Autores Cristianos in Madrid in 1955. Abbreviating the work as *STh*, I cite from the three parts in four sections as Ia, IaIIae, IIaIIae, and IIIa, making use of the standard divisions into question (q.) and article (a.). For example, Ia, q. 1.3 indicates the First Part, the first question, and the third article. Sometimes, for greater precision, I use corp. for the body of Thomas's response, and ad 1, ad 2, and so on for his responses to the objections to his position. Other works of Thomas are cited according to standard abbreviations, a list of which can be found at the end of the book. I have included a number of endnotes to the chapters. These can easily be disregarded by readers who wish to follow the narrative without distraction, but they may be useful for those who wish to pursue aspects of Thomas's thought on specific issues, especially in light of the vast literature on the *Summa*.

Bernard McGinn
Chicago, January 2013

Every civilization has classic expressions. There are some cultural artifacts that come to sum up a period and a style while also becoming part of the common patrimony of human society. In European civilization Shakespeare's plays not only epitomize Elizabethan England, but continue to be read around the world. The same is true of the art of Michelangelo and Leonardo, the music of Bach and Beethoven, the writings of Cervantes and Goethe. In terms of the long Middle Ages (ca. 500–1500 C.E.), when Catholic Christianity was a dominant force, it is not surprising that many of the most famous cultural artifacts are religious. Disputes about which expressions of medieval culture are the most characteristic continue, but few would question that in art the medieval cathedral plays a central role, just as Dante's *Divine Comedy* does in literature. From the perspective of religious thought the *Summa theologiae* of the Dominican friar Thomas Aquinas (1225–74) has a unique place, in terms of both its profundity and its influence. Given its length, few have

ever read the whole of the *Summa*. College gradu-
ates, especially students of religion and philosophy,
may have studied a few selections, but somehow
the *Summa* remains one of the few medieval works,
along with Dante, known to the general public, at
least in name.

This is a brief account of the *Summa theologiae*.
More specifically it is a biography of the *Summa*,
introducing its intellectual gestation in the mind of
Thomas, its structure and contents, and some aspects
of its impact on later history. It may seem foolhardy
to attempt a short book about such a large book. The
Summa is a massive work, containing over a million
and a half words divided into three large parts containing 512 topics (*quaestiones*) and no fewer than
2,668 articles (*articuli*) dealing with particular issues
(some topics are given only two articles; the longest
receives seventeen). In the translation of the English
Dominicans published in the early decades of the
past century the *Summa* takes up 2,565 double-
column pages. Even more daunting is the vast literature that has been devoted to explaining the *Summa*.
Although the work was contentious from the start,
and its history has had ups and downs, the *Summa*
has never lacked for readers and commentators. It has
been calculated that over a thousand commentaries
have been written on the *Summa*, not a few longer
than the original. Commentary, however, scarcely
tells the whole story, because some of the most interesting chapters in the reception of the *Summa* in the

seven and a half centuries since its writing concern thinkers who did not consider themselves followers of Thomas, but who pondered his thought to enrich their own speculation, sometimes in appreciation, sometimes in opposition. Even today, when the age of long commentaries seems over, scores of books and even more articles are published every year dealing with Thomas and especially with what is universally admitted to be his most important work, the *Summa theologiae*.

The following account is selective and personal—one scholar's attempt to present what an interested and curious reader might want to know about the *Summa* and its reception. In thinking about the book, I have been guided by something dear to Thomas and central to what he was trying to do in writing the *Summa*—what he called *sapientia*, that is, wisdom. According to Thomas, wisdom is to be numbered among the "intellectual virtues," or operative habits of the mind. It is the greatest of these because "it deals with the highest cause, which is God." Thomas continues, "And because judgment is made about an effect through its cause, and the same is true about lower causes through the higher cause, so wisdom is the judge of all the other intellectual virtues; it belongs to it to put them all in order. It has a kind of commanding role (*quasi architectonica*) with respect to all the others."[1] Thomas tells us at the start of the *Summa* (Ia, q. 1) that the subject of the work is what he calls *sacra doctrina* (sacred teaching or instruction) and argues that it is a *scientia*, a "science" in the Aristotelian philosophical sense of an organized body of knowledge based on strict deductive reasoning (see chapter 2). But he also insists that *sacra doctrina* is a *sapientia* (q. 1.6), and not just the metaphysical wisdom that Aristotle argued was the judging and ordering habit of the human mind insofar as it philosophically considers the First Cause, but a wisdom that is found *in* God and communicated to humans through revelation. The cultivation of this higher form of wisdom rooted in revealed truth is what the *Summa* is all about. Sometimes this wisdom rooted in faith is supplemented by a third form of wisdom, the *sapientia* that Christians held was one of the seven special graces or gifts of the Holy Spirit, enabling the recipient to have a "connatural" awareness of divine truth and proper action.

Thomas, like other medieval authors, thought that the etymological root of *sapientia* was *sapida scientia*, literally, "tasteful, or savory knowing,"[2] thus emphasizing that *sapientia* has a greater affective, even experiential, quality than abstract deductive reasoning. He also holds that wisdom is its own reward: finding wisdom is not merely instrumental to achieving some other goal. In the prologue to his *Commentary on Boethius's "De hebdomadibus"* he summarizes, "Zeal for wisdom has this privilege, namely that in pursuing its work, it pleases itself even more. . . . Hence, the contemplation of wisdom is like a game for two reasons. First, because a game is enjoyable and the contemplation of wisdom brings the greatest delight. . . . Second, because a game is not ordered to something else but only to itself; this belongs to the delights of wisdom."

The wisdom found in revelation and the wisdom that is the gift of the Holy Spirit go beyond any wisdom we can acquire by our own thinking—they are what Thomas calls "supernatural gifts." They come forth *from* God and are integral in our return *to* God, that is, they are salvific. For Thomas there is a cycle of wisdom, a circular process of emanation and return to God, following the order of the circular model of the creation and return of the universe. This cycle is also written into the plan of the *Summa* (more on this in chapter 2). For Thomas, as for most ancient and medieval thinkers, circular movement was the highest form of motion. As he put it in his other *Summa*, the *Summa contra Gentiles* (*SCG*), "An effect is most perfect when it returns to its source. Hence the circle among figures and circular motion among all the forms of movement are the most perfect, because there is a return to the source in them. For this reason in order that the whole of creation attain its final perfection, it is necessary for creatures to return to their source."[3]

The cycle of wisdom is a useful way of thinking about the production of the *Summa theologiae* in Thomas's mind and the story of its reception. The friar's efforts in creating his masterpiece were generated by wisdom and designed to cultivate and increase wisdom (not just knowledge) in those to whom the book was taught, as well as in its later readers. What follows is my attempt to illustrate the cycle of wisdom that for Thomas Aquinas was the purpose of the *Summa theologiae*.[4]

The World That Made Thomas Aquinas

The intimate relation between culture and religion in the Middle Ages is helpful for understanding Thomas Aquinas. As Bernard Lonergan once put it, "Besides being a theologian and a philosopher St. Thomas was a man of his time meeting the challenge of his time. What he was concerned to do may be considered as a theological or philosophical synthesis but, if considered more concretely, it turns out to be a mighty contribution towards the medieval cultural synthesis."[1] In order to comprehend the significance of Thomas's synthesis, it is helpful to consider three contexts that formed Thomas's life and work: first, the papal reordering of Western medieval Christianity; second, the rise of the university and scholastic theology; and third, the birth of the mendicant religious life, including the Dominican Order to which Thomas belonged.

In early medieval Latin Christianity the bishops of Rome often had little influence over what went on in other parts of Europe. Popes, bishops, and priests were mostly under the control of lay lords, especially the Carolingian and German emperors. In the mid-eleventh century, however, a group devoted to reforming Christian society emerged in Rome, one whose adherents not only argued for freeing ecclesiastics from lay control, but also held that the pope, not the emperor or any layman, had ultimate authority over Christian society. These reformers, of whom the most forceful was Pope Gregory VII (r. 1073–85), set out an agenda for the cleansing of church and society that led to ideological clashes and even armed conflict between the emperors and their followers and Gregory and his adherents. As is often the case with revolutionary movements, several decades of turmoil eventually led to a compromise based on a clearer distinction between what belonged to Caesar and what belonged to God. The Gregorian Reform, by freeing the papacy from lay control, helped spur important advances in the legal, financial, and administrative machinery of the pope and his court. The growth of papal government in the twelfth and thirteenth centuries was not only a material reality, but also a symbolic triumph as the popes came to be seen as the direct masters of Western ecclesiastical structures and the arbiters of Western religious beliefs and values. The Gregorian Reform emphasized the separation between the clergy and the laity, while encouraging efforts to support more effective education of priests. Precisely how much authority the popes had in what today we would call political decisions remained a contentious issue; subsequent conflicts between popes and lay rulers disturbed Europe throughout the later Middle Ages. Nevertheless, no good Christian in Thomas's time doubted the pope's supremacy over the church, and Thomas and his fellow Dominicans were among the papacy's most loyal supporters.

The emergence of the medieval university and its distinctive style of theology, that is, scholastic theology, are also important for grasping Thomas Aquinas's intellectual world. Scholasticism, understood in the broad sense as a structured, "rationalized" interpretation of religious belief, was integrally related to the growth of the university as *the* distinctive institution for higher learning between the late eleventh and the early thirteenth centuries. The eleventh century witnessed the beginnings of a revival in both the monastic and the episcopal schools that had experienced serious decline in the ninth and tenth centuries. The French monastery of Bec, under the leadership of Lanfranc (d. 1089) and Anselm (d. 1109), both later archbishops of Canterbury, became a center of advanced theology. Episcopal schools in Germany (e.g., Cologne) and especially in France (e.g., Chartres, Laon, Paris) acquired reputations as effective places for the education of the clergy. By the mid-twelfth century the episcopal schools of northern France had begun to acquire an organization showing much similarity to modern universities, including structures of administration, basic curricula of teaching, and the employment of famous "masters" (*magistri*) who could attract students on an international level. The stages in the development of the schools in Paris (there were several in the twelfth century) into the full-fledged university which emerged between about 1150 and 1215 are not fully clear, but by the time Thomas Aquinas went to study there in 1245, the university had been flourishing for about a half century.[2]

Many disciplines were taught in the medieval universities, but theology was the highest, "the queen of the sciences," as some put it.[3] This was certainly the case at Paris. But what exactly was the scholastic theology of the twelfth and thirteenth centuries? Scholastic theology is a particular *way* of thinking about belief, done in a special *location*, the formal setting of the university and the lower theological institutions that prepared students for the university. In other words, scholastic theology is distinguished primarily by a method or approach, as well as by a style of teaching.[4] We should not think of the scholastic method as uniform and rigid. Different modes of argumentation—expositive, deductive, inductive, axiomatic, analogical, and more—were all employed by the scholastic masters. These masters used the same materials (the Bible, the Fathers of the church, the councils, papal decrees, etc.); they employed logical modes of argument based directly or indirectly on Aristotle; and they argued to new conclusions. Nevertheless, their ways of arguing and the conclusions they reached were often diverse, so we cannot summarize scholastic theology according to any particular set of teachings, or to a single system of thought. We should rather see it as a rationalized system of ways of appropriating Christian faith in an organized academic setting.

The scholastic theologians were professional educators and rigorous scientists in their pursuit of an understanding of belief. In line with the search for order and logical clarity that marked twelfth- and thirteenth-century society in general, they strove to organize the diversity of patristic theology (the thought of the Christian Fathers of East and West), with its inconsistencies, contradictions, and unsolved problems, into a coherent and teachable model that would not only educate the clergy and instruct the faithful, but also rebut attacks on Christianity both from without (Jewish and Arabic thought) and from within (i.e., heresy). The schoolmen were convinced that there was a reasonableness to faith, albeit they saw this in different ways. In this sense, there was a common purpose to the scholastic endeavor, despite the differences among its practitioners.

The scholastic masters based their curriculum on the Bible, but as taught in formal courses that demanded organized tools for scriptural study and using methods that subjected the text to philological and logical investigation. The earliest great textbook of the medieval schools, composed by different authors in the first half of the twelfth century, was the *Ordinary Gloss* (*Glossa ordinaria*), an immense running commentary on the entire Bible culled from the Fathers, especially Augustine. Glossing, or explaining, the Bible by citing authorities was not new, but the academic context of the professional classroom demanded a new and more extensive kind of textbook. Classroom study of the Bible produced a more positive sense of the importance of the literal meaning of the text, though not to the detriment of spiritual readings.[5]

Education in the schools was based on reading and explaining the text (*lectio*), both of the Bible and of a variety of other textbooks. What was essential to scholasticism, however, was the second academic operation: the *quaestio*, that is, asking what the issues revealed in the texts meant. Aristotle had said that questioning was the essential operation of the human mind, a passage often quoted by the schoolmen. Setting the "question" was a complex endeavor, involving not only attempting to know what could be known about the truths of faith, but also discerning the limits of reason in investigating belief. In studying the Bible and Christian tradition, scholastic teachers encountered a mass of "authorities" (*auctoritates*), that is, positions argued by the early church Fathers and found in ecclesiastical texts. These authorities often seemed to be (or actually were) in conflict, but the need to order church and society sought to bring coherence out of differing viewpoints. Legal scholars led the way at the end of the eleventh century in pursuing a "concord of discordant views," and the early twelfth-century theologians soon followed their example. The first task in working toward the solution of discordant positions was to create textbooks that would gather and organize the data of Christian teaching (often called *Books of Sentences*, that is, compilations of statements of doctrine); the second was to establish principles and procedures that would allow teachers to identify solutions in cases where authorities disagreed. An early example of this was Peter Abelard's *Yes and No* (*Sic et non*), composed about 1122, in which he says, "It is by doubting that we come to investigation, and by investigating that we attain truth" (*Prologue*). The quest for solutions to inherited problems centered on the nature of the *quaestio*. By the mid-twelfth century, one of the masters of this era, Gilbert of Poitiers, put the issue this way: "Not every contradiction makes a question . . . , but where both sides appear to have valid arguments, there you have a question" (*Commentary on Boethius's "De Trinitate"*).

By this time scholastic masters were producing works of linked *quaestiones* on difficult biblical texts or knotty theological issues. The evolution of the *quaestio* was furthered by a variety of factors, especially greater accessibility to Aristotle's logical works (the "Old Logic" had been known for centuries, but the "New Logic" of the *Analytics*, *Topics*, and *Sophistics* was translated ca. 1120–50). Aristotle was not only the master of logic, but also a philosopher who wrote on every aspect of philosophical learning. Scholastic hunger for access to the full Aristotle led to several waves of translations of his corpus between circa 1190 and 1260, a development that had a great impact on Thomas Aquinas.[6] Late in the twelfth century the academic evolution of setting and solving questions evolved into formal "disputations" (*disputationes*), public events where a master and his pupils would debate various aspects of a problem and set forth their solution. In the thirteenth century such disputations became a regular part of every master's job description.

New modes of investigating faith were only half the story. Rational differentiation of teaching operations and new methods of analysis called out for better models of organizing what had been found. How could the masters of the schools summarize this rapidly expanding knowledge for the students who were expected to convey it to the church in preaching? The drive for systematization led to the creation of textbooks and surveys of theology. The theological textbooks of the twelfth century, however much they used new methods of arguing, looked to the patristic past for their organizing principles, thus showing the continuity of Western theology. Augustine dominated early scholastic efforts at creating textbooks. The most successful textbook was produced about 1140 by Peter Lombard, a Paris master and later bishop of the city. Titled *The Books of Sentences* (*Libri sententiarum*), it consisted of four books of theological passages culled from the Fathers with discussions and explanations, arranged according to the Augustinian model (found in *On Christian Teaching*) of the difference between things and signs and between use and enjoyment. Some of the Lombard's early followers toyed with his structure, occasionally anticipating aspects of the ordering procedures found in Thomas's *Summa theologiae*, but these minor adjustments do not seem to have been a factor in Thomas's break with the Lombard's model. By the 1220s the Lombard's *Sentences* had become the dominant theological textbook—a position it maintained for almost three hundred years.

One popular way of describing the scholastic enterprise, "distinguish in order to unite," raises the question, "Unite for what purpose?" What was the ultimate aim of the new carefully articulated form of theology? Some monks, like Bernard of Clairvaux, criticized masters such as Abelard for seeking knowledge only for the sake of knowledge, but the majority of the scholastics insisted that deeper understanding of faith was intended to foster the spiritual life, both of individuals and of the church as a community. This meant that theology had to be not only taught, but also preached. The Paris master Peter Cantor (d. 1197) summarized the different aspects of scholastic teaching as follows: "Learning sacred scripture consists of three things: reading, disputing, and preaching. . . . Reading (*lectio*) is the foundation as it were and basis for what follows. . . . Disputation (*disputatio*) is like the wall in this work and edifice, because nothing is fully understood or faithfully proclaimed unless it has first been broken up with the tooth of disputation. Preaching (*praedicatio*), which these serve, is like the roof that covers the faithful from the heat and storm of vices. Thus, you should preach only after, not before, the reading of sacred scripture and the questioning of doubtful matters through disputation" (*The Abbreviated Word*, chap. 1). Calls for the renewal of preaching grew toward the end of the twelfth century, partly in response to the threat offered the medieval church by heresy, especially dualist heretics called Cathars or Manichaeans. The need for sound doctrinal preaching against heresy was an important factor in the foundation of the Dominican Order, the third context for Thomas Aquinas's life and work.

The Dominicans were part of the religious groundswell of the twelfth and thirteenth centuries that sought to find more effective ways of living the *vita apostolica*, the "apostolic life" of Christ and the first disciples. Medieval monks had seen themselves as following the apostolic life, taking the image of the Jerusalem community described in Acts 4:32 as their model; but the spiritual strivings of nonmonastics that began in the early twelfth century viewed the apostolic life according to the picture of the apostles presented in Luke 10 and similar texts—those who went forth in poverty to preach the Gospel and convert the world. There were many apostolic poverty groups in the twelfth and thirteenth centuries. Some led to the formation of new religious orders that gained papal approval, such as the Franciscans and Dominicans; others, after promising beginnings, came to be condemned as heretical. The reasons for success and failure are not always easy to determine and often seem due to historical accidents or personality clashes.

Francis of Assisi (ca. 1181–1226), born into a mercantile family, experienced a conversion about 1205 and turned to a life of penance, poverty, and service to the poor, especially lepers. Francis's model of apostolic service proved attractive. By 1208 he and a few companions began to form a "brotherhood" of those devoted to poverty, and about 1209 they went to Rome to gain papal approval and the "license to preach everywhere," although their preaching was a matter of moral exhortation and preaching by example. Their new "mendicant," or begging, life expanded rapidly. Francis's contemporary, the Spaniard Dominic Guzman (ca. 1174–1221), took a different path in his founding of the Dominican Order of mendicants.[7] After his ordination, Dominic joined a group around the bishop of Osma in Spain who were reviving the canonical life (i.e., priests living in a monastic way). He and his bishop traveled to France on embassies in 1203–5 and became involved in preaching against the dualist heretics. They became convinced that only itinerant preaching by priests practicing apostolic poverty could counter this danger to the church. Dominic dedicated himself to this work and by 1215 was put in charge of a group of priest-preachers in Toulouse. This "Order of Preachers" (*ordo praedicatorum*) received papal approval between 1216 and 1218. Dominic, a superb organizer, traveled widely to attract followers. From the beginning, the Dominicans were meant to receive the best theological education to foster their preaching mission, so it is no surprise that as early as 1217 Dominic established a house at Paris connected with the university. An insight into the preaching charism of the Dominicans can be found in the *Treatise on the Formation of Preachers* written by Humbert of Romans (d. 1277), the fifth Master General of the order. Reflecting on the relation of study and preaching, Humbert says, "Though the gift of preaching is surely had by God's gift, a sensible preacher still ought to do what he can to ensure that his preaching is commendable by carefully studying what he has to preach."[8] Thomas Aquinas fully agreed.

Creating the *Summa theologiae*

CHAPTER 2

The Life of Thomas Aquinas

We know a fair amount about the life of Thomas, and several good biographies have appeared over the past half century.[1] While we have considerable information about the details of Thomas's career, given the objective character of his writings, we have almost nothing from him that reveals his inner reflections and feelings. We also need to note that many of the stories about him come from the materials put together for his canonization process,[2] and since hagiography has a different purpose from biography, these need to be used with circumspection. Still, there is much of historical worth in the sources.

Thomas was born in 1225 at the castle of Roccasecca, south of Rome, the son of nobility of the lands of the Emperor Frederick II (1196–1250). His father, Landolph, belonged to the house "de Aquino," hence his name; his mother, Theodora, was an aristocrat from Naples. Thomas, the last of his father's numerous progeny from two marriages, was destined for a career in the church. At the tender age of five his family "offered" him to the famed Benedictine monastery of Monte Cassino, where he was brought up as an oblate destined to become a monk and (according to the hagiographers) future abbot of Monte Cassino, given his family's status in the region. Thomas was thus raised in a monastic environment: the religious life and liturgy formed him in his most impressionable years. Although he preached in his own south Italian dialect, he taught, wrote, and probably often thought in Latin.

Noting his intellectual precocity, when he was about fourteen (ca. 1239) the abbot of Monte Cassino sent Thomas to study at the new university of Naples founded by Frederick II in 1224—the first state university. Here he absorbed the seven liberal arts and began the study of some of Aristotle's works under the guidance of first-rate scholars, such as Peter of Ireland. The Dominicans were also present at the university and Thomas began to feel a strong attraction to the new order. Sometime around the age of sixteen (ca. 1242) he joined the Dominicans, much to the chagrin of his family. Their opposition led the Dominicans to attempt to spirit him away from Naples to Paris, but he and his companions were overtaken and captured by some of Thomas's brothers north of Rome. Thomas spent well over a year in a kind of house arrest, resisting his family's attempts to make him abandon his Dominican garb, and (at least as recounted in the early sources) his chastity, by introducing a comely young woman into his room—whom he drove off with a burning fireplace log.[3] He also profited intellectually from the forced detention, reading the whole of the Bible and beginning to study Peter Lombard's *Books of Sentences*.

By 1245 his family relented and Thomas was back on the road to Paris. From 1245 to 1248 the young friar studied in Paris at the Dominican convent of St. Jacques. He probably took courses under the other great intellect of the thirteenth-century Dominicans, the theologian and polymath Albert the Great (ca. 1200–1280). Albert's capacious mind embraced scientific interests in botany, zoology, and mineralogy, not of concern to Thomas, but he was also a profound philosopher and theologian, important for encouraging the study of Aristotle and of the "Dionysian corpus," the body of difficult theological works attributed to the "Dionysius of the Areopagus" mentioned in Acts 17:16, but actually composed by a Syrian monk around 500. Thomas accompanied Albert to Cologne in 1248, when the Dominican Order called on Albert to set up a new general house of theological studies (*studium generale*) for the Dominican convents of Germany. Thomas remained there as Albert's assistant between 1248 and 1252. Although Thomas does not mention Albert by name in his writings, the fact that he spent seven years with this master had a profound influence on his thought. It is likely that it was in Cologne that Thomas began to act as a "Biblical Bachelor," teaching introductions to biblical books. His *Commentary on Isaiah* probably dates to this period and is his earliest theological work.

By 1252 Thomas was in his late twenties and his character and genius were evident. Albert advised the Dominican Master General to send him back to Paris to complete his theological studies. The hagiographical accounts give a consistent picture of the young Italian friar. Physically, Thomas was tall, corpulent, and balding. Personally, he was humble, mild, and gentle. What struck his contemporaries most was his silence and his tendency to what his contemporaries called "abstraction." Thomas lived in his head, constantly occupied with thinking through theological issues, or "rapt in contemplation," as the hagiographers understood it. He often seems not to have noticed what was going on around him. An illustrative story of Thomas at this stage is the account of "the dumb ox" (*bovus mutus*) from his Cologne years. According to this tale, Thomas's reticence to speak up in the classroom led some of his classmates to refer to him by this title. Albert, however, was impressed by Thomas's grasp of his lectures on the Dionysian *Divine Names* and commissioned the young friar to take part in a public disputation. Thomas's role as Albert's assistant was to summarize arguments for and against the thesis, but when he offered his own distinction to settle the issue, Albert pressed him vigorously about his solution. Satisfied by his answers, Albert exclaimed, "We call him a dumb ox, but he will still give out such a bellowing in doctrine that it will sound throughout the whole world!"[4]

Another aspect of Thomas's life noted by the sources, both in his youth and later, was his devotion to prayer. He prayed even more than required by the Dominican daily round of liturgical and personal prayer, and is said to have often had recourse to prayer when confronted by difficult theological problems. The sources are also unanimous that Thomas was characterized from his early years by remarkable powers of memory. He seems to have had what we would call today a photographic memory, that is, he was able to recall word by word almost everything he had ever read. We may take this with a grain of salt, but when one considers the tens of thousands of texts, long and short, cited throughout his works in an age before modern bibliographic or electronic search engines, it is hard to deny that Thomas had phenomenal powers of recall.

The quiet, prayerful, brilliant young friar began to teach at Paris in 1252 as a "Sentence Bachelor" responsible for teaching and writing on the four *Books of Sentences*. Thomas's massive *Writing on the Books of Sentences* (*Scriptum super libros sententiarum*) was his first major work (it contains almost a million and a half words). Although positions advanced here were later superseded in the *Summa theologiae*, the testimony of William of Tocco and others on the impact his novel lecturing and writing had in Paris in the early 1250s is telling:

> When he was made a bachelor and had begun to pour out in his lectures what he had beforehand chosen to hide in silence, God infused such great knowledge into him . . . that he was seen to surpass even all the masters [of theology], and, by the clarity of his teaching, to move the students to love of knowledge more than others did. In his teaching he argued new articles; he found a new and clear way of deciding questions; he brought in new proofs in scholastic determinations to the extent that no one who heard him teaching new matters and settling doubtful questions with new proofs doubted that God had enlightened him with a new kind of illumination.[5]

Although there is doubtless a bit of *parti pris* in one Dominican writing for the canonization of another, it is hard to doubt that Thomas's Parisian students were "blown away," as we say, by his brilliance and originality.

Thomas remained teaching in Paris from 1252 to 1259. After several years expounding the *Sentences*, he was promoted by papal letter to the position of *magister in sacra pagina* (Master of the Bible) in the spring of 1256 and had to prepare an inaugural lecture and dispute several questions over two days. The lecture, discussing Psalm 103:13 ("Watering the mountains from his places on high, the earth will be filled from the fruit of your works"), gives us a sense of how the young friar understood his vocation. Thomas says that all wisdom comes down from God to water the mountains, that is, the teachers of doctrine. Hence these "mountains," the masters of sacred scripture, are called to be high in the quality of their lives, enlightened in their lecturing, and well-armed to refute errors. In communicating true teaching to make the earth (i.e., their hearers) fruitful, they do not depend on themselves. "God communicates wisdom by his own power," says Thomas, "and so he is said to water the mountains by himself; teachers can only communicate wisdom in a ministerial role."[6] What is worth noting is not only Thomas's emphasis on the communication of wisdom, but also the humility with which he approached his calling.

Thomas and his contemporary, the Franciscan Bonaventure of Bagnorea (1217–74), who had been promoted in 1253, were not accepted into the lists of the masters until 1257, and then only under papal pressure. The reason was the quarrel that had erupted between the friars and the nonmendicant masters at the university in the 1250s, a controversy that had a considerable impact on Thomas's thought and career. Religious novelty was often suspect in the Middle Ages, and although the mendicants had won papal support, they had many opponents. The favors the mendicants gained from the popes, both in pastoral care and at the university, provoked a group of secular masters led by William of St. Amour to attack them from 1252 on. The Franciscans and Dominicans were accused of setting dangerous precedents and of being religious hypocrites, even of being the false preachers and forerunners of Antichrist who were predicted to arise at the end of the world (Matt. 24:11–12). The peril was real: the supporters of the secular masters threatened the houses of the friars to the extent that King Louis IX had to call out the royal archers to defend them. On the intellectual side, both orders turned to their rising young stars to answer the charges. In 1256 and 1257 Bonaventure and Thomas wrote defenses of the mendicants, upholding their status as true followers of the "apostolic life" of Jesus and the disciples.[7] While Thomas's temperament seems to have been basically irenic, his writings against those who attacked the mendicants, as well as later against the radical Aristotelians, show that in polemical situations he could be roused to expressions of anger and exasperation. Nevertheless, Thomas's mode of engagement was always to encourage discussion, not invective. In a passage from a later work in defense of the mendicant life, the treatise *On Perfection* written in 1270, he says,

> If anyone wants to write against what I have said, it would be most welcome. There is no better way to open up the truth and to refute falsity than to answer opponents, as Solomon says, "Iron sharpens iron, and a person sharpens his

friend's face" (Prov. 27:17). God himself, who is blessed forever, will make the judgment between us and them. Amen.[8]

During the period 1256 to 1259 Thomas taught at Paris as one of the two Regent Masters of the Dominicans, disputing and composing his questions *On Truth*, perhaps the most significant of his disputations,[9] as well as works like a *Commentary on Boethius's "De Trinitate*," important for its view on the relation of philosophy and theology. We should remember that Thomas, as a member of the Order of Preachers, also preached. Even though he was an academic and not assigned to a parish, he was required to preach Latin sermons to the university community during the year, and, when in southern Italy, he preached to broader audiences in the vernacular. Only about twenty of Thomas's academic sermons survive, but we have Latin collections of sermons on important religious texts, such as the "Our Father," the "Hail Mary," the "Apostles' Creed," as well as homilies on the ten commandments (probably originally given in Italian). These sermons show Thomas was a strictly doctrinal preacher, but clear, concrete, and easy to follow. He avoided the lively exemplary stories and rhetorical flourishes found in much medieval preaching.[10]

Sometime in late 1259 or early 1260 Thomas returned to the Roman province of the Dominicans, probably first going to his home convent in Naples.

In 1261 he was ordered to the convent at Orvieto north of Rome, which was also the location of the papal court. Thomas was the "Reader of Theology" at this house between September 1261 and September 1265. It was during this time that he brought to conclusion a project he had begun in Paris, what is called in the manuscripts both the *Summa against the Pagans* (*Summa contra Gentiles*) and *The Truth of the Catholic Faith against the Errors of Unbelievers*. In four books (some surviving in his own hand), this work was intended to show that theology could make good use of philosophy in its investigation and defense of revealed truths, both those that have been studied by the philosophers, though often erroneously (books 1–3), and those, like the Trinity and Incarnation, that cannot be attained by reason (book 4). By consensus, this work is Thomas's other great synthesis, along with the *Summa theologiae*. In the second chapter of the first book of the work Thomas expresses his intention with a rare personal tone: "Taking up by divine kindness the task of pursuing the office of a wise person with confidence, although it is beyond my powers, my intention is to make known the truth that the Catholic faith professes to the best of my ability by eliminating the errors against it."

Friar Thomas's intellectual efforts during these four years extended widely. He completed a long *Commentary on Job*, one of his most important biblical works, and at the behest of Pope Urban IV wrote a treatise *Against the Errors of the Greeks* (1263 or 1264), in which he appealed to the Greek Fathers to correct what he considered the errors of contemporary Greeks. It was also at the pope's request that Thomas began one of his most popular works, *The Golden Chain* (*Catena Aurea*), a running commentary on the four Gospels culled from the Greek and Latin Fathers, showing a deep knowledge, unusual for the time, of many Greek writers. Finally, and again at the request of Urban IV, Thomas composed the Mass and Office for Corpus Christi, which was proclaimed as a universal feast on August 11, 1264. Despite some doubts about its authenticity, this collection of readings, prayers, and hymns to the Eucharist (the famous "Pange lingua," or "Sing My Tongue") reveals Thomas's sacramental piety and considerable skill as a poet. On September 8, 1265, the provincial authorities again sent orders to Thomas, commanding him to repair to nearby Rome and the convent at Santa Sabina on the Aventine. It was at Santa Sabina that he began the writing of the *Summa theologiae.*

During the 1260s Thomas made contact with the new and improved translations of many of Aristotle's works by a fellow Dominican, William of Moerbeke, who had spent time in Greece and learned the language well. Older claims about Moerbeke's influence on Thomas are now considered exaggerated, but there is no question that during this decade Thomas deepened his knowledge of Aristotle by beginning to write a series of commentaries on the Greek philosopher. Thomas was to write no fewer than a dozen commentaries on Aristotle in a relatively brief time (ca. 1267–73). In the nineteenth and early twentieth centuries, when Thomas was seen as an "Aristotelian" in outlook, these works were carefully mined to extract an "Aristotelico-Thomistic" philosophy. That view is now disputed, and some have questioned whether we should speak of Thomas as an "Aristotelian" at all (a term he never used). Nevertheless, Thomas knew Aristotle well, cited him extensively throughout his works, and generally followed Aristotle's philosophical views. But we still can ask why Thomas expended so much energy in writing his commentaries, some quite long, on Aristotle's writings.

The answer lies in Thomas's conception of the vocation of the theologian. As he began the writing of the *Summa theologiae* in 1266, Thomas seems to have become more and more convinced that a careful study of the philosophical resources found in Aristotle could help him deepen his thinking on important theological issues, such as the nature of the soul. He may also have been aware of the growing disputes over the use of Aristotle, the "Aristotelian crisis" that began to disturb the University of Paris in the 1260s. Thomas thought that in the midst of debates over the legitimacy of employing Aristotle in theology, it was necessary to correct misinterpretations and to give students a clear and correct understanding of how the "Philosopher" (as he was named in the medieval schools) could be used in theology, as well as the limits of that use.

In 1268 Thomas was called back to Paris to assume one of the two Dominican chairs of theology. This was an unusual privilege, but the Order seems to have become convinced that Thomas's presence at Paris was important in the midst of the conflict over the use of Aristotle and the deeper issue of the role of philosophy in theology. Although the teaching of Aristotle's natural philosophy had been banned at Paris in 1210 and 1215, it proved impossible for both the masters of the arts faculty and the theologians to refrain from employing such a useful intellectual tool, not only in logic, but also more broadly in philosophy. By the 1230s Aristotle was creeping back in, and in the 1240s Albert the Great and others were teaching and commenting on Aristotle and using Aristotelian elements in their theology. Like most medieval textbooks, Aristotle's writings were used within a "commentarial envelope," that is, along with the extensive explanations of the Islamic philosopher Ibn Rushd (1126–98), or Averroes. Aristotle's philosophy, however, especially as filtered through Averroes, conflicted with Christian belief at key points, such as its claim for the eternity of the universe and its denial of personal immortality because of the teaching that there was only one universal Intellect in which all humans participate (monopsychism). Some teachers of Aristotle in the arts faculty, often called "Averroists" (Thomas was the first to use the term) or "radical Aristotelians," presented Aristotle's teachings on these controversial points as necessary conclusions of reason, much to the annoyance of conservative theologians who used such claims to attack any use of Aristotle in theology beyond his logic. These theologians, of whom Bonaventure can be considered the founding father, are often called Neo-Augustinians, because they insisted that Augustine's authority extended equally to both theology and philosophy.

The Dominicans, led by Albert and Thomas, defended a broad use of Aristotle's philosophy as helpful for constructing a reasonable and coherent account of Christian faith, though, of course, they stood ready to convict Averroes, and even Aristotle, of error when their teachings conflicted with revelation. In this heated atmosphere, with Dominican theology under suspicion by the Neo-Augustinians who stressed the dangers of Aristotle, as well as the presence of Radical Aristotelian philosophers who argued that *from the point of view of reason* some important Christian doctrines could not be sustained, the Preachers summoned their premier theological mind back to Paris. Another factor in Thomas's recall was a new flare-up in the attacks on the friars by the secular masters, one that prompted Thomas to write several more defenses of the mendicant life after his return to Paris.

The details of the Aristotelian quarrel cannot delay us here. Suffice it to say that the positions of the Radical Aristotelians, like Siger of Brabant and

Boethius of Dacia, were condemned by Stephen Tempier, the Bishop of Paris, in December 1270, while the opposed theological camps of those who were suspicious of Aristotle (mostly Franciscans) and those in favor of using philosophy, including Aristotle despite his problems (mostly Dominicans), were left to fight it out. Many issues were under contention. Two key differences between Thomas and his opponents, such as the Franciscans Bonaventure and John Pecham, involved Aristotle directly or indirectly. The Philosopher had argued for an eternal universe; Christian revelation taught that the universe was created in time (*in principio*: Gen. 1:1). The Franciscans contended that reason *alone* could prove Aristotle wrong, while Thomas, against most of his contemporaries, argued that the duration of the universe, that is, whether it was eternal or temporal, could not be demonstrated by reason—creation in time is a truth of revelation. A second major issue concerned the unicity of the substantial form of the human person. Thomas held that the soul was the single substantial form of the body; his opponents believed that a number of different forms or souls (vegetative, sensitive, rational), including a "form of corporeity," constituted the human person, something like the layers of an onion. Though there had been differing views about this issue, even in the recent past, by Thomas's time most masters held to a plurality of forms, often citing Augustine (incorrectly) in their favor. The dispute seems arcane to us, but it had implications regarding personal immortality and the status of Christ's body after death that were important to the scholastics.[11] These quarrels, among others, disturbed Thomas's second Paris period and continued to dog his reputation after death.

The dozen years 1261–73 in Italy and France saw Thomas at the height of his powers. A number of incidents recounted by the hagiographers provide us with a sense of what he was like. These tales seem to come in part from the witness of Reginald of Piperno, the friar who was assigned to be Thomas's special companion (*socius*) from as early as 1259 until his death, functioning as the master's helper, secretary, confessor, and (in the case of the absent-minded Thomas) what we might call his "minder." One such story, meant to indicate Thomas's indifference to worldly matters, rings especially true. It seems one day Thomas and some students walked out to St. Denis in the Paris suburbs to reverence the church's relics.[12] On their return, as they sat down looking out at Paris, one of the brethren said, "Master, see what a beautiful city Paris is. Wouldn't you like to be Lord of the city?" "Why," answered Thomas, "what would I do with it?" The student said that he could sell it to the king to build houses for the friars. "I would rather have the homilies of Chrysostom on Matthew's Gospel," responded Thomas. William of Tocco gives some moralizing remarks he ascribes to Thomas about not wanting to be put in a position where his contemplation would be impeded, but the original exchange reveals Thomas's academic obsessions.[13]

In early 1269 Thomas had less than five years of teaching and writing left. They were to be years of almost incredible productivity, because he was not only continuing work on the massive *Summa theologiae*, but also teaching, disputing, and writing commentaries on Aristotle and the Bible at an astonishing rate, not to mention various treatises, short and long. Thomas lived in a tearing hurry—he probably thought he never had enough time. Few great thinkers have produced so much material of such quality in so short a time—quite probably to the detriment of his health. Most of the Aristotelian commentaries come from these years. With regard to the Bible, Thomas wrote long commentaries on the Gospels of Matthew and John, the latter possibly his greatest exegetical work. He also composed two important polemic treatises against his opponents. In 1270 his *On the Unity of the Intellect Against the Averroists* attacked the claim of the radical Aristotelian Siger of Brabant that there is only one Intellect in which all humans participate. In the same year he rebutted John Pecham's argument that reason alone can prove that the world must have had a beginning in *On the Eternity of the World Against the Murmurers*. These polemical writings did not preclude Thomas's obligations of teaching the Bible and conducting public disputations, later put into written form in the

Disputed Questions on the Virtues and a number of his *Quodlibetal Disputations*.

Thomas returned to Italy in the spring of 1272. On June 12 the Roman province assigned him the task of setting up a new *studium generale*. Thomas chose his home convent for this house of studies. Thus, his life as a Dominican, begun in Naples thirty years before, was to see its last chapter there. In the First Canonization Inquiry of 1319 we are given a picture of Thomas's daily routine by a layman Nicholas Fricia, who used to hear Mass daily in the Dominican church and attend Thomas's lectures:

> Very early in the morning Thomas would say his Mass in the chapel of St. Nicholas, after which ... he heard another Mass, and then, taking off his vestments, at once began his teaching. This done, he would set himself to write or dictate to his secretaries until the time for dinner [midday]. After dinner he went to his cell and attended to spiritual things until siesta, after which he resumed his writing. And so the whole of his life was directed to God. It was the common view ... that he had wasted scarcely a moment in his lifetime.[14]

Thomas had little more than a year left in Naples, but it was filled with the same intense activity that marked his second professorship in Paris. He pursued the writing of the Third Part of the *Summa*, possibly begun in Paris. He continued to lecture on the Bible, to dictate a variety of other works, and, of course, to organize the new house of studies. Along with the ongoing work on the *Summa*, it seems that most of the commentaries on Paul were either given or revised in Naples, as well as his commentaries on the Psalms. As always, Thomas continued to write treatises, both by request and for his own interests. Among the most important of these was the *Compendium of Theology*, a doctrinal synthesis organized around the theological virtues of faith, hope, and charity that he wrote for Friar Reginald. He seems to have begun this in his time at Rome, finishing off the chapters on faith. Now he took up the chapters on hope, but death was to preclude completing the work.

Thomas did not get to finish the *Summa* either. On December 6, 1273, something happened that ended his writing career and seems to have hastened his death three months later. The hagiographical sources provide us with considerable detail about these months, but leave us with many questions. Several sources indicate that when Reginald noted that Friar Thomas was even more abstracted than ever and asked him why he was no longer writing, Thomas replied, "Reginald, I cannot, because all I have written seems like straw to me."[15] He also expressed the wish that the only thing left for him was death. What is certain is that the immensely productive Thomas never wrote another word and that he seemed even less aware of his surroundings than ever. What had happened?

The medieval lives put the end of Thomas's writing down to a mystical experience, a foretaste of the vision of God in heaven, the *visio beatifica* that Thomas had written about so brilliantly. God showed Thomas that however much he strove to penetrate the meaning of the beatific vision, his efforts were nothing more than the merest hint of an explanation (something Thomas himself would not have contested). A mystical experience? Perhaps. Modern investigators, noting the incredible pressures Thomas had been under for the past five years, think that there was also a psychological and/or physical component to the event of December 6, that is, a mental breakdown of some sort, or even a stroke.[16] These medieval and modern explanations are by no means mutually exclusive.

As is customary with medieval hagiography, we are given a detailed picture of Thomas's last months to demonstrate the sanctity of his death. In January 1274 he received a command from Pope Gregory X to attend the planned council at Lyons, where Thomas's expertise would have been useful for the attempted reconciliation with the Greek Church. Thomas, Reginald, and their companions began the trip north. During the trip, he struck his head against a fallen tree encumbering the road and was injured (Thomas's impaired mental state may have had something to do with this). According to one story, Reginald tried to cheer Thomas up by saying that he and his Franciscan contemporary Bonaventure would probably both be made cardinals at the council. Thomas was not amused and told him to be quiet.[17] Providence had other things in store for Thomas. Within a few days, he felt the end was near and asked to be taken to the nearby Cistercian monastery of Fossanova south of Rome in order to be found "in a religious house" when the Lord came for him. Many stories surround his last few days at Fossanova, because the medieval impetus for saint-making was already at work. Two of these stories seem characteristic of the friar: Thomas's profession of faith in Christ's presence in the Eucharist, and his express wish to leave his many writings to "the holy Roman Church, to whose judgment I submit all my teaching." Thomas died on the morning of March 7, 1274.

The fact that Thomas Aquinas was seen by his contemporaries as a saint as much as he was a theologian is evidenced by the fate of his body, the relic of a holy man. The Cistercians of Fossanova were delighted to be in possession of Thomas's body and to have so many stories about his last days. They soon began to receive pilgrims anxious to pray at the grave of the saint and possibly receive succor and healing. Miracle stories began to spread.[18] Afraid that the Dominicans might steal or commandeer the body with papal approval, they moved it several times and may have cut off the head to keep it should this happen. We know that at one exhumation Thomas's hand was removed and given to one of the saint's sisters, though the thumb was later presented to the Dominicans. As ghastly as this all sounds, it fits medieval reverence for the relics of holy men and women. At some time after Thomas's canonization, the remains were boiled down, and the more transportable bones were eventually given to the Dominicans, who laid them to rest in their church at Toulouse in 1369.

Thomas's Writings

Thomas Aquinas's literary output is immense. Granted that his whole life from his mid-twenties was committed to teaching and the composition of works for the training of students and the elucidation of theological issues, it is still impressive to survey the thousands of pages and many millions of words he left to posterity. Although specimens of the friar's crabbed handwriting (called the *littera illegibilis*, or unreadable hand) exist, most of his works were dictated to secretaries. (Thomas was said to have been able to dictate different works at the same time, something like a chess master playing several games simultaneously.)[19] We have already mentioned some of Thomas's writings in the biographical sketch above, but it will be helpful to provide an overview of the more than a hundred works ascribed to him, ranging from short treatises, letters, and sermons, to exhaustive commentaries and immense syntheses.[20]

Something like the devotional triptychs that graced medieval altars, Thomas's works can be divided into three major sections, or panels. In the center stands the panel of his large syntheses; various commentaries form one outside panel, disputed questions and treatises, short and long, the other. The syntheses include the early *Writing on the Books of Sentences* of Peter Lombard, the *Summa contra Gentiles*, and especially the *Summa theologiae*. Many would also add the unfinished *Compendium of Theology* here. Medieval theology was always based on *lectio*, that is, commentary on authoritative texts. Thomas's earliest synthesis was officially a comment on the Lombard, but, like most scholastics, for him the *Books of Sentences* had come to serve as a springboard for his own treatment of theological issues. But Thomas was also a powerful commentator in the strict sense. Foremost among these works are his expositions of books of the Old and the New Testaments. Although formerly neglected, they are now considered basic for understanding his theology and have come in for much study in recent decades. His lengthy commentaries on Aristotle are also important, especially for understanding his position in the quarrels over the Philosopher in the thirteenth century.

Correcting the older Neoscholastic emphasis on the purely Aristotelian basis for Thomas's thought, recent investigators have turned their attention to the Platonic element in his work, for which his commentaries on Platonic (better, Neoplatonic) texts are of importance, especially two works of the late antique Christian Neoplatonist Boethius (*On the*

Trinity, and *On the "De hebdomadibus"*), as well as on *The Divine Names* of Pseudo-Dionysius and on *The Book of Causes*. Although Thomas never wrote any commentaries on Augustine, the African bishop, deeply indebted to Platonism, was his most important theological source, and hence many studies of the Augustinianism of Thomas have recently been produced. The recovery of the Neoplatonic element in Thomas's thought has been a major achievement of the past generation of Thomist scholarship, but it runs the risk of repeating the mistake of the nineteenth- and early twentieth-century scholars who confidently asserted that Thomas was a "real" Aristotelian. Truth told, Thomas absorbed much from both Aristotle and the Neoplatonists, but he would not have been happy to be termed either an "Aristotelian" or a "Neoplatonist"—nor, of course, a "Thomist."

The third panel of the triptych consists of Thomas's investigations into special themes and issues, both individual problems and major themes of theology and philosophy. Thomas's most penetrating discussions of many issues are often found in his *Disputed Questions*, especially those he directed to what he felt were the most difficult intellectual problems: What is truth? What is evil? What is the power of God? What is the soul? What are the virtues? These disputed questions can be thought of as the workshops, or laboratories, where Thomas and his students studied the intricacies of speculative questions, weighing the arguments pro and con before establishing the positions he expressed in a briefer form in his syntheses, especially in the *Summa theologiae*. Where there is overlap between the arguments in the *Summa* and those detailed in the *Questions*, the same position is usually adapted, but the *Questions* give us a fuller sense of why Thomas chose a particular position after considering and rejecting alternative views. One of the delights of studying Thomas is to follow his argumentation from the exhaustive analyses in the *Questions* to the crisp summaries of the *Summa*.

The other part of the third panel consists of Thomas's treatises. Most of these were occasional pieces, responding to issues of the day and often written in response to requests from powerful ecclesiastical or political figures who could not be refused (approximately twenty-six works fit this description). One can imagine that Thomas was not particularly happy with some of these distractions from his more important work, but he did his duty. A few of these treatises have had an impact on various disciplines, such as philosophy, where the early treatise *On Being and Essence* proved to be very popular (close to two hundred manuscripts). Another popular philosophical work is his response to Siger of Brabant, *On the Unity of the Intellect Against the Averroists*. In theology his treatise *On the Articles of the Faith and the Sacraments of the Church*, written in the 1260s, gained a wide audience. In the early fourteenth century Bartholomew of Capua, who had known Thomas at Naples in the 1270s, began to collect stories about him and read his works. Bartholomew compiled a catalogue of the friar's writings in which he noted, "These writings can be read with ease and profit by everyone, according to his mental capacity. Hence we find even laymen and people of modest intelligence desiring to possess copies of them."[21] This is strong testimony to Thomas's impact on a wide readership.

The Plan and Purpose of the *Summa theologiae*

Imagine a warm autumn afternoon in the year 1266 in Rome on the Aventine hill overlooking the city from the ancient church of Santa Sabina.[22] The church belonged to the Dominican Order, having been granted to Dominic and his followers by Pope Honorius III in 1221. On this afternoon Thomas Aquinas is engaged with his secretaries on a new kind of theological initiative, the book that will be called the *Summa theologiae*, that is, an ordered synthesis of theology (the title may not be original but appears in most early copies).[23] During his time on the Aventine Thomas and his scribes would complete the *Prima Pars* of the *Summa*, consisting of 119 questions and 584 articles dealing with God and creation. In late 1268 Thomas was called back to Paris to serve as Dominican Regent Master for a second time. He would remain there from 1268 until the spring of 1272, teaching and writing at a pace that is still hard to imagine, finishing the largest, or second, part of the *Summa*. This *Secunda Pars* was so massive that Thomas split it into two subsections, the *Prima Secundae* of 114 questions and 619 articles, dealing with the role of human acts in general in attaining beatitude, and the *Secunda Secundae* of no fewer than 189 questions and 916 articles on human acts in particular in the return process. Considering the *Summa* alone, Thomas's productivity during these Paris years is impressive. According to one calculation, he must have written about twelve pages of modern print every day to finish the *Secunda Pars*.[24] Back in Italy by spring 1272, Thomas worked on the third part of the *Summa*, managing to finish 90 questions and 549 articles, dealing with Christology and most of the sacraments, before the incident of December 6, 1273, when he stopped writing.

Thomas's *Summa theologiae* is one of the great works in the history of Christian thought.[25] In its original form (i.e., minus the *Supplementum* of 99 questions on the final four sacraments and eschatology compiled by his students from his earlier writings), its three parts consist of no fewer than 2668 articles, or mini-disputations. Each of these mini-disputations follows a standard form: (1) posing the question to be examined (e.g., "Was it fitting for the Word to be incarnated?"), (2) giving a series of arguments against the answer that Thomas intends to support (usually three or four, sometimes more), (3) citing an authoritative text (most often from the

Bible) as the proof or principle of the position to be taken (called the *sed contra*), (4) arguing for his own position in what is called the body of the article (*corpus*), and finally (5) answering the objections one by one. Sometimes Thomas's position entails making distinctions concerning the question to be examined, exploring in what sense it can be affirmed and in what sense denied. The fact that whole books have been written about single questions shows that even in its small sections the *Summa* invites detailed commentary and, quite often, disagreement about Thomas's meaning. We need to ask why, for whom, and to what purpose Thomas Aquinas undertook this project. Putting the *Summa* into the historical context of Thomas's life helps us get a better sense of what he had in mind.

Christian theology, or *sacra doctrina* as Thomas preferred to call it in the *Summa*, treats not only eternal truths about God, but also the historical *opera reparationis*, or works of salvation (Ia, q. 1.7), so it is not illegitimate to ask how Thomas's own story provides insight into what he sought to do in his great work. Few, if any, Christian theologians made more of the fact that our thinking about God is ineluctably tied to our existence as embodied subjects; human attainment of truth is in and through the body and its senses, though the intellect abstracts the intelligible form from the matter perceived by the senses (Ia, q. 85.1). The tall, corpulent friar sitting in Santa Sabina, later in the Dominican convent in Paris, and finally in Naples, was enmeshed in a rich history that helps us understand what his intentions were in writing the *Summa*.

Thomas's growing reputation in the 1260s led to an unprecedented move on the part of his own Roman Province. The Dominican model of educating future preachers, confessors, and teachers was organized according to a carefully orchestrated program of study begun in the individual houses or priories, continued in the provincial houses of study (*studia provincialia*), and completed for the most gifted students in the *studia generalia*, the houses of graduate studies, of which Paris was the most important.[26] When the Roman Province summoned Thomas to Santa Sabina in 1265 it seems to have intended him to set up an unprecedented *studium personale*, a house of study centered on his own teaching, with special privileges granted to students he selected who were guaranteed financial support from the order. He was also allowed to terminate their studies if he judged they were not measuring up.[27]

In his Roman teaching Thomas was required to comment on selected theological texts and to hold disputations at announced times. Ordinarily, he would have lectured on Lombard's *Sentences*, and an incomplete fragment of a second commentary on that work gives evidence of this.[28] Thomas, however, soon abandoned this in favor of beginning the *Summa theologiae* in 1266. Some of the commentaries and disputations he pursued during his years at Santa Sabina seem to have been chosen to help him think through issues he was treating as he progressed in the writing of the *Summa*. For example, Thomas commented on Dionysius's *Divine Names* at Rome in two courses (1265–66 and 1266–67). This theological work, the Magna Carta of apophatic, or negative, theology, profoundly shaped his understanding of divine unknowability found in the early questions of the *Prima Pars*.[29] Similar correlations between the progress of the *Summa* and works from Thomas's later teaching in Paris and Naples are also illuminating.

Did Thomas actually teach the *Summa* at Rome? Authorities disagree, and the best answer is that we really do not know.[30] We are not even sure if Thomas gave public lectures on the *Summa* at Paris and Naples; he did, after all, have many other teaching obligations, especially at Paris. Thomas and his select group of students and scribes may have had more than enough to do as they labored away on the new textbook within the context of their own discussions and dictation. On the other hand, Thomas was insistent on the centrality of teaching and the need to create a new model of theological education, so we may wonder why he would not have put this model to the test.

It is clear from the "Prologue" to the *Summa* that Thomas was quite aware of the break he was making from standard pedagogy and his reasons for doing so. He says,

We have considered that beginners (*novitios*) in this teaching have been much put off by what has been written by different authors; in part by the proliferation of useless questions, articles, and arguments; in part by the fact that what is necessary for them to know for this science is not set out according to the correct order of learning (*secundum ordinem disciplinae*), but by what is required for commenting on texts, or for what provides material for disputations; and finally in part because the frequent repetition of these matters causes boredom and confusion in the hearers (Ia, *prologus*).

The reference to "beginners" has proven puzzling. How could a text so condensed, so brilliant, so deceptively clear be intended for "beginners"? It all depends on what we mean by beginners. It seems most likely that with regard to his immediate audience, the novices Thomas addressed are not to be understood as total beginners in the study of theology, but rather, in accord with the two levels of Aristotelian *scientia*, they are those who have absorbed the general principles of the understanding of faith through their previous courses on Aristotle, the Bible, and perhaps even Peter Lombard's *Sentences*. In other words, these medieval novices are something like modern graduate students in theology.[31] Thomas intends for them to deepen their knowledge and to learn how to introduce other beginners, the faithful, into a better understanding of belief through their preaching and teaching. Thomas may also have had in mind Dominican convent lectors whose task it was to introduce the majority of friars to basic theology.

Given Thomas's sense of the originality of his project, we can address the meaning of the composition of the *Summa* by asking what Thomas intended by creating this new model for theological education, and how he conceived of the content and structure of the work. Neither of these questions has a straightforward, or uncontested, answer.

When we ask what Thomas intended, we must remember that he was first and foremost a teacher. The vocation of a Dominican friar was not to sit in the chair of a *magister* solving questions for the sake of clever answers with an eye to writing texts for the ages, but rather to form students, especially young friars, to become theologians capable of giving good sermons, hearing confessions with accurate theological knowledge, and, if necessary, refuting heretical attacks on Christian faith. A recent line of interpretation of the *Summa* has argued that the *Summa* was intended primarily as a new way of presenting moral theology to Dominican students who would soon go forth to preach and hear confessions.[32] In this view, Thomas was reacting to the older Dominican theological formation that concentrated on a moral theology centered on the description of virtues and vices, or on canon law prohibitions of sinful actions. Thomas wished to create a better theological understanding of Christian morality based on the human desire for happiness, as we find it laid out in the *Secunda Pars*. Thomas realized from the start, however, that it would not be enough just to write another textbook on moral theology, but that sound moral teaching could be successful only if grounded in an integral theology.

This "moral view" of the *Summa* explains much, but it may be misleading insofar as some might be tempted to think that the *Prima Pars* is a mere introduction and the *Tertia Pars* a kind of addendum on Christ and the sacraments. We may well imagine that Thomas came to see the need for a new kind of theological textbook by reflecting on what his Dominican charges needed to become preachers and confessors, without concluding that moral theology was the only or controlling factor in his vision for the work. Rather, as the passage cited above from the *prologus* suggests, Thomas had come to think that the whole of theological education was out of whack. To see why this was so, we need to look at what Thomas meant by invoking the *ordo disciplinae*, or pedagogical order, and why he called the subject matter of his work *sacra doctrina*, not *theologia*. To that end we need to take a close look at the first question of the *Prima Pars*, titled "The Nature and Extent of Sacred Teaching," which introduces the subject matter of the whole.[33]

Sacra doctrina ("sacred instruction") emphasizes the act of teaching, that is, training minds to master the modes of thinking necessary to command this particular subject matter—what the church believes and teaches. In his earlier (1259) commentary on Boethius's treatise *On the Trinity* Thomas had discussed the difference between two kinds of *theologia*, that of the philosophers, also called *scientia divina* or *metaphysica*, and the *theologia Christiana* based on revelation.[34] By 1266 he had altered his terminology. Although he still occasionally speaks of *theologia*,[35] his choice of *sacra doctrina* to describe the content of his new work is significant. *Theologia* deals with a set of propositions concerning God—*scientia* as a set of conclusions. *Sacra doctrina*, however, emphasizes instruction, the generation of *scientia* (*scientia in fieri*), that is, how a master trains students to learn a subject according to proper pedagogy, or the *ordo disciplinae*.[36] As he put it toward the end of the *Prima Pars*, "A master not only makes his students knowledgeable, but also teachers of others" (q. 103.6). This emphasis on teaching does not mean that content is overlooked, but if we abstract the *Summa* from the context of instruction and make it a text merely for reading and laying out a set of conclusions about God, we risk perverting Thomas's purpose, whether he intended the work more as a manual for teachers, or as an actual class text for reading and commentary.

The ten articles that constitute the first question on *sacra doctrina* reveal the originality and precision of Thomas's mature thinking on understanding faith. In order to grasp the nature of a discipline one needs to know three things: whether the discipline exists (*an sit*), the nature of the discipline (*quid sit*), and finally the method of the discipline (*de modo arguendi*). Thomas investigates the first issue in article 1. Articles 2 through 7 take up the nature of *sacra doctrina*, while articles 8 to 10 consider its mode of arguing.[37]

The first article asks, "Whether it is necessary to have another form of teaching besides the philosophical disciplines?" If the many branches of philosophy investigate everything that can be known, culminating in metaphysics (the divine science or theology that investigates God), what need is there for any other kind of knowing or teaching? The key to the answer, as everywhere with Thomas, is teleology—the end or goal determines the means to attain it. For Thomas, the final cause is "the cause of causes," so if we can demonstrate that something is demanded by the final cause, we have the most strict kind of demonstration (*demonstratio propter quid*). Thomas does not mount a philosophical argument for God as the final end here, but, in keeping with the nature of the discipline he is investigating, cites scriptural authorities: Isaiah 44:4, proving that God is the final goal that surpasses our understanding, and 2 Timothy 3:16, concerning scripture as divinely revealed for our instruction and salvation. Since God is the goal of humanity as the "good surpassing nature" (*bonum supernaturale*), and no finite human mind on its own natural powers could ever attain the saving knowledge that leads to the "supernatural" God who is above all that we can know, God reveals this knowledge to humans so that they can be saved.[38]

Sacra doctrina is absolutely necessary for salvation. Its saving content, Thomas contends, must include not one, but two kinds of truths about God—those that surpass reason, such as the Trinity, and also those, like the existence of God, that are open to reason but that are difficult to attain and can be known only imperfectly. Without knowing that God exists, the whole edifice of sacred teaching would collapse, but the same is true for God as Trinity. While Thomas thought that some metaphysicians, even non-Christian ones, had attained knowledge of the existence of God, and while he knew that most humans had some imperfect conception of god or gods, all these convictions, from the crudest to the most profound, had no saving power. This insight displays the grandeur and the misery of metaphysics: it is the highest form of *human* knowing and natural contemplation, but it is always flawed and without salvific effect.

Thomas uses reason and philosophical modes of arguing throughout the *Summa*, but it is not a work of philosophy, or even of philosophical theology. The *Summa theologiae* is fundamentally a work of doctrinal theology, however much it makes use of philosophy and philosophical theology (i.e., metaphysics). Since *sacra doctrina* is a true science, it needs to make use of both reason and faith, of philosophical and theological argumentation. If philosophy and theology are necessary, however, they are not equally necessary—only revelation and the faith based on it are salvific. Etienne Gilson expressed the nature of this form of theology well when he said, "[I]t is of the essence of the theology called 'scholastic' that it appeals freely and widely to philosophical reasoning. Because it draws on faith, it is scholastic *theology*, but because of its distinctive use of philosophy, it is *scholastic* theology."[39]

Thomas could not be clearer about the necessity of *sacra doctrina* for salvation, but his insistence raises a problem that again emphasizes the centrality of teaching and learning. If *sacra doctrina* is needed for salvation, does this mean that Thomas and his advanced students alone will be saved? What about the illiterate old lady in the back of Santa Sabina during morning Mass?[40] Will she have to pay tuition and start a theology degree (*per impossibile* for a woman in the medieval church)? This *reductio ad absurdum* shows that all believers have to share in the activity of *sacra doctrina*, that is, in being instructed and learning the truths of faith to the best of their abilities. Since the source of *sacra doctrina* is God's infinite self-knowledge, the difference between all our finite receptions of such knowledge, whether those of Thomas and his students or of the old lady in the back of the church, sink into insignificance. For Thomas what they (and we) all need to have in order to be saved is willingness to be instructed.[41]

The stage is now set for Thomas to investigate what kind of discipline *sacra doctrina* is. Article 2, which asks whether *sacra doctrina* is a science in the Aristotelian sense, has been the source of much discussion. Many thirteenth-century theologians had investigated whether theology could be considered a science, usually answering that it was so only in an imperfect sense, because of several difficulties in squaring the strict Aristotelian notion of science as found in the *Posterior Analytics* with the Christian "understanding of faith."[42] Thomas was one of the few who insisted that *sacra doctrina* was indeed a real *scientia* in the Aristotelian sense. We must remember that this is far from the modern sense of empirical and experimental sciences. For Aristotle *scientia* is "sure knowledge through causes," best illustrated by rigorously deductive disciplines, such as mathematics or geometry, that is, organized bodies of knowledge in which indisputable principles lead by syllogistic reasoning to necessary conclusions.[43] Thomas argues that *sacra doctrina* does, indeed, meet the essential requirements of Aristotelian *scientia* in that it argues from principles revealed by God, shows the causal relationships among revealed doctrines, and demonstrates new conclusions. It is important to note, however, that Thomas does not cite Aristotle as his authority for this, but rather Augustine on "wisdom as the science of human and divine matters" (*On the Trinity* 14.1.3), already hinting that *sacra doctrina* is a science because it is wisdom.

Thomas goes beyond Aristotle in how he conceived of *scientia* as an analogous term, one capable of being understood in a variety of ways. Several shifts in meaning from Aristotle are important to note. For example, Aristotle allowed for "subalternate" sciences where one body of knowledge depends on premises known from another (e.g., for ancient thinkers music depended on mathematics), but *sacra doctrina* is a science subordinate to a science we cannot know, namely, God's supreme, non-discursive self-knowledge. Another difference is that in Aristotle's view sciences were either speculative (i.e., contemplative) or practical, directive of action; for Thomas, *sacra doctrina*, although primarily speculative, is both speculative and practical (a. 4), that is, it deals essentially with God and secondarily with human actions.

It is clear that *sacra doctrina* is an unusual "science," one that while it may fulfill the basic premises of Aristotle's view of science as sure knowledge, stretches Aristotle beyond what he would have recognized. The reason for the unique nature of sacred teaching is manifest in article 6, which is the key to the whole first question: "Is Sacred Teaching Wisdom?" In order to understand why *sacra doctrina* is wisdom we can turn to Thomas's earlier *Summa contra Gentiles*, where he offers a reflection on the vocation of the Christian theologian in the first two chapters. Considering the theologian as the student of divine wisdom, Thomas says,

Just as it is proper for the wise person especially to meditate on the truth about the First Principle and then to consider other things, so too he has to attack the falsity contrary to it. This is why it is fitting that the twofold task of the wise person (*sapiens*) is proclaimed by the mouth of [Divine] Wisdom in the passage cited (Prov. 8:7): to speak the divine truth that has been meditated upon . . . , and to attack any error against truth. (*SCG* I.1)

All of Thomas's writings, but especially the *Summa theologiae*, were attempts to fulfill his vocation of a teacher of wisdom.

Wisdom is a fundamental theme of biblical teaching enshrined in the Wisdom literature of the Old Testament and especially in Paul in the New Testament, who often contrasts the wisdom of this world with the wisdom of God (Rom. 8:6; 1 Cor. 1:20–21, 2:6). Aristotle had identified wisdom in the philosophical sense as the habit of knowledge that puts things in their proper order (*sapientis est ordinare et non ordinari*).[44] Augustine also made much of wisdom, especially in books 12 and 14 of *On the Trinity*, where he treats the superiority of divine wisdom over the science of earthly things. Thomas's teaching on wisdom is an original synthesis of these sources.

Sacred teaching is wisdom, Thomas says, because "it belongs to the wise person to order and to judge" (art. 6), a constant theme in his teaching.[45] Ordering and judging are rooted in the essential act of wisdom, that upon which all its ordering and judging depend, namely, contemplation: "Wisdom considers [i.e., contemplates] the very object of happiness, the highest intelligible being" (IaIIae, q. 66.5, ad 2).[46] Aristotle analyzed wisdom as the intellectual habit that orders and judges all the disciplines, but Thomas also found this teaching in Paul, who said, "The spiritual person [i.e., the wise person] judges all things" (1 Cor. 2:15).[47] A science does not establish its own principles, but as *sapientia* sacred teaching not only establishes its principles from revelation, but also explains them insofar as it can, defends them against attack, and judges the first principles and conclusions of the other sciences. As wisdom, it also orders all the principles and conclusions of revealed teaching, connecting the truths to each other and arranging them in the best way to achieve the goal to which they are directed, the pursuit of eternal happiness.[48] Since wisdom puts things in order, and all ordering is effected in relation to an end or goal, the whole teleological structure of the *Summa* is the expression of Christian *sapientia*. Such wisdom follows the model of the most perfect form of movement, circular motion, by beginning from principles, arguing to conclusions, and returning to the principles with deeper understanding.

Article 6 says that *sacra doctrina* makes use of philosophical *sapientia*, which judges and orders things from the perspective of the highest cause as known from creatures (Rom. 1:19 is cited), but that it depends primarily on the higher wisdom of the Bible "in relation to what is known to God alone about himself and communicated to others through revelation." Thomas, however, distinguishes this form of revelation-based wisdom that can be cultivated by study (*per studium*) from the highest wisdom, the gift of the Holy Spirit, by means of which believers come to know divine matters through connaturality (art. 6, ad 3). There are then three kinds of *sapientia*, with the *sapientia* that is *sacra doctrina* occupying a middle position between the acquired natural wisdom of metaphysics and the infused wisdom that comes from the Holy Spirit.[49] The *ordo doctrinae* and *ordo disciplinae* set forth in the *Summa* form two sides of a sapiential ordering based on the revelation found in the Incarnate Word.[50] *Sapientia* is central to understanding what Thomas intended in writing the *Summa*.[51]

Having established that *sacra doctrina* is the highest sapiential science, Thomas turns to how sacred teaching functions in the last three articles in question 1. Science in the Aristotelian sense is "argumentative" (*argumentativa*), that is, it uses reason to argue from principles to conclusions. *Sacra doctrina* is also argumentative (art. 8), but once again with a twist. For Aristotle, the supreme human science of metaphysics depends on principles that are inherent in human knowing, such as the principle of contradiction (i.e., that something cannot be both true and false under the same aspect at the same time). Human thinking presupposes but does not prove these essential truths. In the case of sacred teaching, however, the human mind accepts truths on the authority of God revealing, although these truths are by no means self-evident (e.g., that the one God is a Trinity of persons). Having accepted these truths as principles, the sapiential theologian can defend them against attack and deduce further insights for believers. Hence, sacred teaching argues in different ways for different audiences. In the case of those who do not accept revelation, it can only rebut arguments that the articles of faith are totally incoherent or contradictory. With those who accept revelation, but have gotten some of its teaching wrong ("the heretics" for Thomas and his contemporaries), it can argue from the articles held in common to the truth of those under dispute. Finally (and most important), for believers, its arguments make manifest the implications of faith, following the Augustinian program of "faith seeking understanding."

Thomas sums up his conviction about the importance of reason for *sacra doctrina* in the famous formula: "Since grace does not take away nature but perfects it, it is necessary that natural reason serve faith, just as the natural movement of the will serves charity" (a. 8, ad 2).[52] A passage in his *Commentary on Boethius's "On the Trinity"* puts it this way: "Those who make use of philosophical teaching in sacred teaching by redirecting them to the use of faith do not mix water with wine, but rather change water into wine."[53] Thus, in its form of arguing sacred teaching uses both principles based on authority, which in the case of a revealed science are the strongest kind, as well as principles from philosophy, though these are external and only probable in matters of faith. Nevertheless, in each mode Thomas makes use of the mind's inherent dynamism to move from premises to conclusions. What he does not advert to in this discussion, perhaps surprisingly given its importance throughout the *Summa*, is the distinction between arguments concerning revealed truth that can be considered necessary (*ex necessitate*) and arguments from fittingness (*ex convenientia*). For example, it is a revealed premise that Jesus Christ is fully God and fully man. Hence, it follows by *logical* necessity that Jesus must have both a divine will and a human will. However, there is no necessary proof for the fact of the Incarnation itself. God did not have to become man. Given that the Incarnation is revealed in the Bible, however, *sacra doctrina* allows the believer to explore fitting reasons for why God chose to take on human nature.

Finally, *sacra doctrina* is scriptural, that is, it is based on the authority of God found in the Bible (aa. 9–10).[54] Thomas uses *sacra doctrina* and *scriptura* interchangeably in question 1. If God's revelation is the efficient cause of sacred teaching and salvation the final cause, the instrument revelation uses to convey this knowledge is the Bible, the written word of God. Here another problem surfaces. Sciences in the Aristotelian sense make use of textbooks that are rigorously logical (think of Euclid's *Elements*), but the Bible is filled with stories and metaphors—scarcely a "scientific" book. But, Thomas responds, it is quite fitting for God to use metaphors and corporeal language in conveying his message, both out of necessity because the Bible is directed to all people (not just philosophers), and because it is useful for drawing people to the knowledge of higher intelligible realities through lower sense images (a. 9). But there is an even deeper reason, as shown by the two citations of Dionysius that appear in article 9. Dionysius was aware not only that metaphorical language was necessary out of condescension to our human way of knowing by concrete realities and images, but also that it was important for indicating God's transcendence. Employing philosophical terms like being and goodness and the like might tempt the theologian to think that these concepts can give us knowledge of God's essence. No, says Thomas, this kind of philosophical language "Tells us more about what God is not than what he is; likenesses of the things that are farther away from God give us a truer sense that he is beyond what we say and know of him" (a. 9, ad 3). The true wisdom of the theologian is to know that he or she does not know. Paradoxically, the fact that *sacra doctrina* is essentially scriptural also shows that it is fundamentally negative.[55]

Sacred teaching mediates the transformation of the pictorial language of the Bible into an intelligible scientific account through biblical interpretation. Thomas briefly discusses this in article 10,[56] where he notes the traditional four ways of reading the biblical text, the literal (i.e., what God intended by these words), and the three spiritual senses built upon the letter (the allegorical concerning Christ and the church, the moral concerning human action, and the anagogical pertaining to heaven). He insists that the key to reading a text is the "intention of the author" (*intentio auctoris*). But God is a unique author, because God alone can write on two levels. The words he communicates through the human author as instrument have a literal meaning, and, insists Thomas, the "letter" of the text is often a metaphor that needs to be decoded (e.g., when the Bible refers to "God's arm" it is signifying his power). But the spiritual meanings are also part of God's intention because only God, who controls history, can bring it about that certain things (events, persons, etc.) described in the Bible have meanings that indicate other realities. Nevertheless, Thomas insists that in the practice of *sacra doctrina* arguments (in the true, deductively necessary sense) should be drawn only from the literal sense. This should not be treated as a kind of exegetical straightjacket, because it is clear that Thomas maintained that because human meanings cannot exhaust the divine truth, at least some biblical passages could have a number of literal meanings. Furthermore, Thomas's "literalism" does not preclude all use of spiritual readings in *sacra doctrina*, and he employs a number of spiritual interpretations throughout the *Summa*. Strictly speaking, it seems that such citations should be considered arguments from fittingness (*ex convenientia*), not from necessary deduction.

The modern reader of the *Summa* will be hard put to think of the book as scriptural, because Thomas's use of the Bible is far from our own way of interpreting scripture. However, the Dominican cites scripture more than any other source over the course of the *Summa*, not only in the authorities quoted in the *sed contra* sections of the articles that are the basis for his arguments, but also in his explanations, arguments, and responses. Thomas did his theology with the Bible at hand (or in his head), and he insisted that the Bible be read ecclesially: "Faith inheres in all the articles of belief because of one mediation, namely because of the First Truth proposed to us in the scriptures understood according to the church's correct teaching" (IIaIIae, q. 5.3, ad 2). When we turn to his biblical commentaries for further elucidation of his hermeneutical practice, once again we enter a foreign world, because Thomas is little concerned with the narrative or rhetorical structure of the scriptural books the way that modern biblical scholars are. Rather, he seeks to bring out the doctrinal intelligibility of the revealed message (the *propositum*) by organizing the chapters of the biblical books into comprehensive patterns, especially through what he called "the division of the text," which teased out (some might say "imposed") a scientific structure on the biblical narrative. This process of making the stories and metaphors of the Bible scientifically clear, more evident in some commentaries than others, is foreign to modern exegesis, but it reveals three essential principles for understanding Thomas's view of *sacra doctrina*. The first is that holy teaching is always fundamentally biblical. The second is that the nature of the Bible as God's words directed to humanity must be narrative and metaphorical. The third (the one that we do not share today) is that the role of the *magister in sacra pagina* is to transform biblical narrative and metaphor into a form of articulated scientific discourse to reveal its intelligibility. Thomas's notion of *sacra doctrina* is paradoxically always both scientific and scriptural. As he put it in his *Quodlibetal Question* VII.6.1, "Sacred scripture was divinely handed on for this purpose: so that through it the truth necessary for salvation might be made manifest to us."

What, then, is the order of the sapiential teaching of *sacra doctrina* set forth in the *Summa theologiae*? This is a question that looks easy to answer, given the linear and carefully articulated structure of the work, but it is one that has proven to be a bone of contention.[57] The issue is important, however, because both the order of what is to be taught (*ordo doctrinae*) and the order of how to teach and learn it (*ordo disciplinae*) were crucial to Thomas's decision to write a new theological textbook. The two forms of ordering are in reality two sides of the same coin.

In thinking about the ordering of the *Summa*, it is helpful to distinguish between what have been called the "micro-structures" and the "macro-structures" of the work.[58] The ordering of the *Summa* is evident on both levels, that is, on the micro-level in how Aquinas marshals axioms, principles, definitions, distinctions, divisions, reasons, causes, and questions to attain conclusions that are the starting points, or principles, for further explorations. One of the dominant features of the work is the constant internal cross-referencing by which Thomas builds later arguments on earlier conclusions.[59] The relationship of principles to arguments and conclusions, inherent in the logic of the scholastic *quaestio*, reached a culmination in the *Summa*. "Each question," says Bernard Lonergan, "called for a statement of principles of solution and for the application of the principles to each of the authorities invoked. But a series of questions on a single topic, such as *De Veritate, De Potentia, De Malo*, demanded a coherent set of principles for all solutions on that topic, while a *Summa* needed a single set relevant to every question that might be raised."[60] Hence, the inherent ordering of the smallest micro-structures shapes the articles that are grouped into questions, and questions clustered into topics, or what have been called treatises (Thomas did not use this term), such as the "Treatise on Law," or the "Treatise on Christology."

This sapiential ordering is also evident on the level of the most general "macro-structure," that is, the overall plan that Thomas had in mind, especially in dividing the *Summa* into three parts. In 1939 Marie-Dominique Chenu proposed a solution to how the work is structured that has a good textual foundation in the *Summa*.[61] At the beginning of question 2, Thomas says that "the principle intention of this sacred teaching" involves not only God as he is in himself, but also as the beginning and end of creatures, especially rational creatures. Therefore, "with a view to laying out this teaching we will first treat of God; second, of the movement of the rational creature to God; third, of Christ, who, as man, is the way for us in journeying to God." This description of the three parts reflects the model of *exitus-reditus*, that is, the flowing out of all things from God and their eventual return to him, a model Thomas had already appealed to in his *Writing on the Sentences*.[62] Actually, by speaking first of "how God is in himself," and then how God is both the source and the goal of all things, Thomas seems to be implying a threefold, originally Neoplatonic, model that he would have known through the writings of Pseudo-Dionysius, comprising (1) God in God-self; (2) the *exitus*, or procession of creatures from God; and finally (3) the *reditus*, or the return of creatures to God. Both God in himself and the procession of creatures from God are found *primarily* in the *Prima Pars*, while the return of all things to God is spread over the *Secunda*

Pars and *Tertia Pars*. This view has won considerable acceptance, although it has had its critics.[63] However, it should not be applied in a rigid fashion. First of all, God's creative power and his role as the end of all things are found throughout the *Summa*. Furthermore, the *exitus-reditus* model does not preclude the presence of other structuring themes at work in the book, such as the various kinds of causality, the role of Divine Goodness, the notion of exemplar and image, and the forms of grace. In sum, we might say that several overlapping structural principles are at work in the *Summa*, each providing insight into the mind of Thomas.

The organization of the *Summa* has been criticized, notably by those who question whether the triple paradigm threatens to reduce *sacra doctrina* to an abstract philosophical account having little contact with the history of salvation revealed in the Bible. Other critiques come from those who note that the *Secunda Pars* with its great length seems almost to submerge the other parts, as well as from those who have wondered if Thomas's teaching about Christ, the core of Christian theology, appears to be a kind of afterthought to the basic structure. Nevertheless, understanding the *Summa* as based on the cycle of emanation and return helps tie much of Thomas's theological work together, from the *Writing on the Sentences* to the *Summa*. In his earliest synthesis Thomas had already referred to the coming forth from and return of all things to God as a key theological principle, but the structure of the Lombard's work did not allow him to use this great circle (*circulatio vel regiratio*) as a structuring principle.[64] Thomas also refers to the *exitus-reditus* model in other works.[65] The *Summa contra Gentiles* seems to depend on it, though in a less evolved way than the later *Summa*.[66]

For Thomas this circular motion reveals God's sapiential ordering on the most universal level. To think of the *exitus-reditus* model as primarily philosophical and Neoplatonic, as some have argued, is a modern view that Thomas would not have shared. What else does scripture teach but how all things were created by God and are directed back to him as their final goal? What else does Christ mean in the Apocalypse when he says, "I am the Alpha and the Omega, the first and the last, the beginning and the end" (Apoc. 22:13)? Furthermore, the Dionysian *Divine Names* that Thomas was teaching at the same time he was writing the *Prima Pars* was the foremost Christian, quasi-apostolic, source for the triple pattern of (1) God in God-self, (2) God as producing all things from his Goodness (*exitus*), and (3) God as the universal goal of *reditus*.[67] Thus, the *exitus-reditus* model had a good scriptural and Dionysian pedigree that would have recommended it to Thomas.

What about the history of salvation and the role of Christ? Once again, we must beware of anachronism or of importing our problems into Thomas's world. Just because the Dominican chose not to follow the mode of presenting Christian faith according to a narrative historical paradigm, such as that of the "work of creation/work of restoration" (*opus creationis/opus recreationis*), does not mean that he thought the order of *sacra doctrina* excluded an integral role for sacred history. Rather, it has been argued that the *exitus-reditus* schema in its inner structure is by definition open to history, even determinative thereof.[68] For Thomas, there was no conflict between the best mode of teaching (*ordo disciplinae*) and the *ordo rerum*, or structure of saving history. Both were expressions of divine *sapientia*, and both were integral to the fabric of the *Summa*. Aristotle's view of *scientia* excluded temporal events; Thomas's *sacra doctrina* necessarily included the events of the course of salvation as recounted in the Old and the New Testaments, though historical events revealed their scientific intelligibility only in the light of revelation. This is why the argument *ex convenientia*, that is, from fittingness, plays such a large role in the *Summa*, especially in the treatment of Christ and the sacraments.[69] The free events that constitute the history of salvation do not proceed from necessary causes, but when God brings them about, we can see how fitting they are in the light of *sacra doctrina*.

This perspective may also help us in responding to two of the other questions addressed to the structure of the *Summa* noted above: Why is the *Secunda Pars* so quantitatively dominant? And why is Christology, the teaching about Christ, placed at the end, instead of being foregrounded? We need not agree with Thomas's decisions here, but we can at least appreciate the reasons he had for making them. The moral interpretation of the *Summa* answers the first question by noting Thomas's intent to train preachers and confessors, but this need not exclude a deeper view. For Thomas, the historical situation within which we are called to participate in the *sacra doctrina* necessary for salvation is the present time in which we must practice virtue and avoid vice as we direct our lives toward the goal of human existence, the beatific vision. Despite its length, its intricacy, and its at times numbing detail about many issues no longer relevant, the *Secunda Pars* is a treatise on how to live and how to guide others in living. How far we might want to adopt Thomas's structure for living today, or to replace it with something new, are valid questions, but these do not affect why Thomas put so much effort into the *Secunda Pars*.

In the case of Christology, Thomas would probably have been surprised at objections to his placing Christ in the *Tertia Pars*. As he says in the Prologue, "Because our Savior the Lord Jesus Christ, . . . showed the way of truth to us in his very self through which we might attain the happiness of eternal life by our rising again, it is necessary that as the fulfillment of the whole business of theology (*ad consummationem totius theologici negotii*), after the consideration of the final end of human life and the virtues and vices, our treatment of the Savior himself and his gifts to the human race should follow."[70] Thus, Thomas clearly thought that the *Tertia Pars* was a culmination, not an afterthought. The immense *Secunda Pars* about attaining the final goal of human living would mean nothing without Christ, who makes it all possible. The last part is the best part, in Thomas's view.

A Tour of the *Summa theologiae*

CHAPTER 3

The basic structure of the three parts of the *Summa theologiae* has been laid out in chapter 2. The present chapter is, in essence, a guided tour of its contents. No survey of the *Summa* can pretend to convey the richness of Thomas's exposition and the wealth of the distinctions, qualifications, insights, arguments, and conclusions he brings to the thousands of theological issues and problems he treats. In what follows I try to give a sense of the range of doctrines considered and to sample a few of the important sections in some detail. This chart gives an initial overview of Thomas's *sacra doctrina* and a sense of the sequential arrangement of each of the parts.

The Structure of the *Summa theologiae*

Prima Pars, Ia (1266–68)

1. Introduction: *sacra doctrina* (q. 1)
2. Proving God's existence (q. 2)

3. How God exists (qq. 3–13)

    a. Essential attributes (qq. 3–11)

    b. How God is known (q. 12)

    c. How God is named (q. 13)

4. Divine operations (qq. 14–26)

    a. God's knowledge (qq. 14–18)

    b. God's will (qq. 19–24)

    c. God's power (q. 25)

    d. God's beatitude (q. 26)

5. The Trinity (qq. 27–43)

    a. The procession of the divine persons (q. 27)

    b. The divine relations (q. 28)

    c. The three persons (qq. 29–43)

       — Persons in general (qq. 29–32)

       — Persons in particular: Father, Son, and Spirit (qq. 33–38)

       — Comparisons of the persons (qq. 39–43)

6. The production of creatures from God (*exitus*) (qq. 44–119)

    a. The notion of creation (qq. 44–46)

    b. The various kinds of creatures (qq. 47–102)

       — Creatures in general (q. 47)

       — Creatures in particular (qq. 48–102)

          * Good and evil (qq. 48–49)

          * Spiritual creatures, or angels (qq. 50–64)

          * Corporeal creatures (qq. 65–74)

          * Mixed corporeal and spiritual creatures, i.e., humans (qq. 75–102)

    c. Providence (qq. 103–19)

Secunda Pars, IIa (1268–72).
The return of creatures to God

Prima Secundae, IaIIae.
Human acts in general in the return process

1. Introduction: Beatitude as the goal of humanity (qq. 1–5)
2. Human acts in themselves (qq. 6–48)
    a. Acts peculiar to humans (qq. 6–21)
    b. Acts common to humans and other animals, i.e., passions (qq. 22–48)
3. The principles of acts (qq. 49–114)
    a. Intrinsic principles: Powers and habits
        — Habits in general (qq. 49–54)
        — Habits in particular (qq. 55–89)
            * Good habits, i.e., virtues (qq. 55–70)
            * Bad habits, i.e., vices (qq. 71–89)
    b. Extrinsic principles: God as
        — Instructing man through Law (qq. 90–108)
        — Aiding man by Grace (qq. 109–14)

Secunda Secundae, IIaIIae.
Human acts in particular in the return process

1. Acts pertaining to all conditions of humanity (qq. 1–170)
    a. Theological virtues
        — Pertaining to the intellect: Faith (qq. 1–16)
        — Pertaining to the will: Hope (qq. 17–22) and charity (qq. 23–46)

b. Cardinal virtues
- — Prudence (qq. 47–56)
- — Justice (qq. 57–122)
- — Fortitude (qq. 123–40)
- — Temperance (qq. 141–70)

2. Acts pertaining to some or given in a special manner (qq. 171–89)

a. Graces gratuitously given, i.e., spiritual charisms (qq. 171–78)

b. The active and contemplative lives (qq. 179–82)

c. Various ecclesiastical offices (qq. 183–89)

Tertia Pars, IIIa (1272–73).

Christ as the way, or the consummation of the theological task

1. Christ in himself (qq. 1–59)

a. Introduction: The fittingness of the Incarnation (q. 1)

b. The mode of the union (qq. 2–15)

- — The union and the Person assuming (qq. 2–3)
- — The human nature assumed (qq. 4–6)
- — What was co-assumed (qq. 7–15):
    - * Christ's grace (qq. 7–8)
    - * Christ's knowledge (qq. 9–12)
    - * Christ's power (q. 13)
    - * Christ's weaknesses of soul and body (qq. 14–15)

c. Consequences of the union (qq. 16–26)

- — Concerning Christ himself (qq. 16–19)

— Christ in relation to the Father (qq. 20–24)
— Christ in relation to us (qq. 25–26)
  d. The mysteries of Christ's life and death
     (qq. 27–59)
     — Christ's birth (qq. 27–36)
     — Circumcision (q. 37)
     — Baptism (qq. 38–39)
     — Life in the world and miracles (qq. 40–45)
     — Passion (qq. 46–52)
     — Resurrection and exaltation (qq. 53–59)
2. Christ active in the sacraments (qq. 60–90)
  a. Sacraments in general (qq. 60–65)
  b. Sacraments in particular (qq. 66–90)
     — Baptism (qq. 66–71)
     — Confirmation (q. 72)
     — Eucharist (qq. 73–83)
     — Penance (qq. 84–90)

Supplementum, Supp. 99 qq., put together by
Thomas's disciples after his death, mostly drawn from
his earlier *Writing on the Sentences of Peter Lombard*
  1. The sacraments in particular, continued (qq. 1–68)
    a. Penance, continued (qq. 1–28)
    b. Extreme unction (qq. 29–33)
    c. Holy orders (qq. 34–40)
    d. Matrimony (qq. 41–68)
  2. The last things and eternal life (qq. 69–99)
    a. The resurrection of the body and last judgment
       (qq. 69–91)
       — The place of souls after death (qq. 69–72)

— The signs of the last judgment (qq. 73–74)
— The resurrection itself (qq. 75–78)
— The condition of the resurrected (qq. 79–87)
— The last judgment (qq. 88–91)
b. Heaven (qq. 92–96)
c. Hell (qq. 97–99)

The *Prima Pars*

After discussing *sacra doctrina* in article 1, the *Prima Pars* begins with Thomas's teaching about God and includes sections on the divine essence in itself (qq. 2–26), the Trinity of Persons (qq. 27–43), and the procession of creatures from God (qq. 44–119). Like a series of Chinese boxes, each of these sections opens up to reveal other boxes and yet smaller boxes within. In investigating many of the doctrines treated in the *Summa*, Aquinas follows a pattern of asking three questions: (1) *whether* the thing in question exists (*an sit*); (2) *what* the thing is (*quid sit*); and (3) *how* the thing functions (*qualis sit*). Thus, the section on the essence of God deals with three issues: whether God exists (q. 2); how God exists, "or rather, how God does not exist," as Thomas tellingly puts it (qq. 3–13); and finally how God acts (qq. 14–26).[1]

Analysis I. The God Question (Ia, qq. 2–13)

Question 2 of the *Summa*, with its "five ways" (*quinque viae*) or proofs, for the existence of God, is perhaps the most read portion of the whole book. What was

Thomas trying to do in the three articles that make up this brief question? Many argue that he was constructing a demonstration in what we today call philosophical theology, that is, a natural proof of God's existence. Others contend that the *Summa* is not a philosophical exercise as such but rather a series of reflections based in revealed truth on the role of reason in faith. This is why at the start Thomas cites a biblical, not a philosophical authority, Exodus 3:14, "I am who am" (q. 2.3). A second point of contention is whether or not Thomas is in fact giving his own proofs for God's existence. There is disagreement here, too, as some contend that he is not so much providing his own proofs as reflecting on the types of arguments philosophers have made for God's existence.

It is important to pay attention to the location of the five modes for arguing for God's existence in the structure of question 2. Thomas begins (art. 1) by ruling out any a priori, or self-evident, proofs for God's existence, that is, demonstrations based on the nature of the term God or on the mind's ability to conceive of truth as demanding a "First Truth." Thomas insists that God's existence is self-evident to God (*quoad se*), but not to the limited human mind (*quoad nos*) that cannot know the divine essence. Here Thomas is taking a stance against some important strands in Christian thought. The second article rules out the opposing error of fideism, the view that God's existence can be affirmed on the basis of faith alone because of its superiority to reason. Thomas contends that while we cannot prove God's existence by demonstrating *why* God must exist, because we do not know God's nature, we can still demonstrate *that* God exists from his effects. In article 3 then, he investigates "whether God exists" through five ways, or lines of argument.

In investigating five arguments for the existence of God, Thomas follows previous philosophers—especially Aristotle—but the arguments are condensed and adapted for his purposes. Each of the five ways follows a similar structure. Thomas begins from observations about the world around us, then investigates the nature of the phenomenon by invoking metaphysical principles. In the first way, for example, Thomas argues that change cannot be fully understood in the realm of physics alone; it demands a metaphysical explanation. Change—that is, a transition from potentiality to actuality (e.g., the transition from being cold to being hot)—demands a catalyst of change outside the being that is changing, because "a thing in the process of change cannot itself and in the same way be both the cause of motion and what is moved; it cannot change itself. Everything that is changed [in this sense] must be changed by something else." With regard to necessary causes, where the cause of change must be presently active for the change to take place (e.g., the stick has to be present for it to move the stone), Thomas argues that an infinite regress of causes is impossible. He therefore concludes that there must be "a First Cause of change, which everyone calls God."

A full explanation of Thomas's five ways of proving God's existence is beyond the purview of this book. Each has elicited a large literature, with many Thomists upholding the validity of the arguments, and other philosophers and theologians denying them.[2] Since the five ways reflect the arguments of previous thinkers,[3] some students of Thomas have wondered if there is a more properly "Thomist" proof, either implicit in them, or developed in some other place in Thomas's writings. Such questions cannot delay us here. It is important to note, however, that the five ways must be seen within the perspective of the whole program of the *Summa*.

Having determined "that God is" (*an sit*), Thomas turns to exploring "what God is" (*quid sit*) in questions 3 to 13. The exercise is paradoxical, because God is not a "what," that is, a being like any of the beings we can know and define. God does not fall under the general notion of being (*ens commune*) at all. Thomas again reminds us that he treats God from the perspective of revealed truth by citing John 4:24, "God is spirit" (q. 3.1). The questions that follow in this part of the *Summa* are exercises in the logic of speaking about the unknowable God.

The key to Thomas's doctrine of God is found in question 3 on the divine simpleness (*simplicitas*). Everything we know in the created world has some kind of composition, for example, the composition of parts in a body, the composition of formal and material principles, and the composition of essence and existence—that is, between what something is and the fact that it is. (Knowing what a dinosaur is does not mean that dinosaurs *have* to exist, as we know from experience because there are no more dinosaurs.) God is not a body, nor any kind of composite thing, because there is no difference between God and whatever things we truly ascribe to him, such as divinity, life, goodness, and so on. God *is* his goodness. In article 4 Thomas poses the question, "Whether in God essence (*essentia*, i.e., what God is) is the same as his act of existence (*esse*)?" He answers in the affirmative. Every being whose essence is *not* its existence—that is, every being that does not *need* to exist—must have its existence caused by a being that necessarily exists. Since God is the First Cause of all, "it is impossible . . . that his existence is one thing and his essence another." Thomas continues, "Because existence is the actuality of every form and nature . . . , it is necessary that existence itself (*ipsum esse*) be compared to the essence that is different from it, as act is compared to possibility." Whereas in Aristotle's universe all beings were composed of possibility for a form and its actuation, in Thomas's universe, by contrast, the relations of possibility and actuality in creatures are rooted in a deeper distinction, namely, the difference between the God who *must* be, because *what he is* is nothing other than his existence, and all other things, which need not have been, but have been called into being by God's creative will.

For Thomas, when we think about the world we are confronted by the question, "Why is there anything?" One might be tempted to reply, "Who cares? That's just the way it is." Thomas, of course, does care. His search for ultimate answers led him to conclude that all the beings we know need not have been. They are, in other words, contingent. But the fact that they *do* exist requires a being whose essence (what it is) is identical with existence (it is), and that such a being is one and the same as the God of Exodus 3:14, who said, "I am who am." God, therefore, is not the highest of *beings* in a hierarchy of good, better, and best within the category of "being in general." Instead, he is totally outside any genus or hierarchy of being (q. 3.5) in a realm beyond our ability to conceptualize. Thomas is far from subscribing to the view that theologians later called "ontotheology," that is, the notion that God can be spoken of within the categories we use for other beings.[4] As Etienne Gilson and others have shown,[5] for Thomas ultimate reality is not substance, or the One, or essence, or some other of the transcendental terms explored by philosophers. The pure act of existence is not a concept, a property or an attribute. Rather, it is what we affirm when we make the judgment *that* God is.[6] In this sense, questions 3 to 13 of the *Prima Pars* are an exercise in transcendental tautology in which we learn that our attempts to capture the absolute simpleness of God in human language simply cannot apply to God. Because there is no difference in God between his essence and his existence, or between his perfections and his nature, all statements such as

"God is good" or "God is perfect" can be reduced to the formula, "To be God is to be." In Thomas's view, the wisdom of *sacra doctrina* is not learning more of *what* can be said about God, but in coming to appreciate more and more fully the mystery of God's unknowable existence by exploring how language falls short of knowing or naming God.

Further on in this initial God section of the *Prima Pars* (qq. 4–11), Thomas conducts a survey of the traditional "divine names," that is, terms or predicates ascribed to God. Here he takes up a theme explored by early Christian thinkers, especially Pseudo-Dionysius. Thomas distinguishes between the negative names (God's lack of composition, lack of end, lack of change) and positive ones (God's perfection, goodness, omnipresence, eternity, and oneness).[7] God's absolute simpleness, states Thomas, expresses his transcendent difference from created reality, while naming God as the perfection of all perfections shows that he is immanent in his creation.[8] The different expositions in this section of *Prima Pars* each reveal something of the richness of Thomas's theology of the divine names.

Thomas caps his treatment of the divine essence with two questions of great import. Question 12 explores how we can be said to *know* God, that is, the modes in which our intellect relates to knowledge of God, while question 13 asks what exactly we do when we *name* God. Question 12 begins by noting that because God is infinite, we can never know

God essentially, that is, the way he knows himself, although faith teaches us that our "natural desire to know the cause from the effect" means that our final happiness rests in the vision of God. Nor can we know God through any created likeness or illumination. Even the vision of God in heaven, although it will involve a direct beatifying sight, will not be a comprehensive vision in which we will see God as God sees God. Here Thomas also denies that anyone in this life could see God's essence save by a brief miraculous exception, and closes by arguing that in our present limited condition grace grants us higher knowledge of God than reason does.

Question 13 is a reflection on speaking about God as simple, perfect, good, one, and the like. What rules ought to govern such speaking, and what do they tell us about the limits of language about God? What terms are appropriate for speaking about God? Thomas begins with the issue of whether any names could really fit God. Thomas approaches the question by invoking a central motif of his thought, the three modes of predicating terms of God. "Because God cannot be seen by us in this life through his essence, he is known by us through creatures, [1] insofar as he is their source, and [2] by way of eminence [i.e., as surpassing them all], and [3] by negation." Here he takes exception to the negative view of Maimonides, according to which all true statements about God are essentially negative, such that names like "goodness" can signify only that God is not like the evil or privation found in created things. Thomas, on the contrary, holds that words indicating perfections—like goodness—really do signify *that* God is good, but also that the *manner* of God's goodness goes beyond anything we could ever know. To say that God is living, for example, "signifies God as the source in whom life pre-exists, although in a higher way than we can understand or signify." Certain words (e.g., goodness and wisdom) can be used of God directly (*proprie*), and not just because God is the cause of these realities in creatures. "Words like this signify the divine perfection, but imperfectly, just as creatures represent him in an imperfect way." Although these names/words can be used properly of God, what does this mean given the imperfection of all our terms in relation to God? How is radical imperfection compatible with proper predication? At this point Thomas introduces an important distinction: "In the names we give to God there are two things to be considered, first, the perfections themselves, such as goodness, life, and the like, and the second, the mode of signifying" (a. 3 corp.). What Thomas means is that we can be sure *that* goodness is true of God, but that we have no idea of *how* transcendent goodness is realized in God. Once again, there is no knowledge of God's essence, or of the perfections that are identical with it.

Thomas's line of argument reaches its culmination in article 5, which asks, "Whether things said of God and creatures are expressed univocally?" Univocal speaking means that when we use a term like "being" of God and a creature we are using it in one and the same way (i.e., both God and creature are beings). Equivocation, on the other hand, means that the same word (e.g., "tart") is used of two totally different things, that is, a dessert and a woman of dubious repute. Thomas argues against both these positions, defending the middle path of analogy: "words of this kind [i.e., perfection terms] are spoken about God and creatures by way of analogy, that is, according to a kind of proportion." Thomas's teaching on analogy has been the subject of a large literature.[9] He employed analogy as a tool for talking about God and God's relation to creatures—for saying how God and creatures are "differently the same." The sameness resides in the fact that both God and creatures are affirmed as truly good; the difference is based on the fact that we can understand how creatures are good, but not how goodness is transcendentally realized in God. Speaking by way of analogy is central to the *Summa*. Many of the more than two thousand articles that follow make use of analogy, because any time we use words both of God and created reality, they have to be employed in an analogical way.

Having finished his consideration of God's essence (*quid sit*), Thomas turns to how God acts in questions 14 to 26, that is, how God knows and wills. With his treatment of God's nature as one then completed, the next major section of the *Prima Pars* (qq. 27–43) treats God as Trinity. Thomas insisted that revelation teaches two kinds of truths: those that are accessible to human reason, but with difficulty, and those that surpass the powers of reason. Among the latter is the doctrine that the one God is a Trinity of persons.[10] The Trinity was central to the Christian reading of both the Old and the New Testaments. Thomas's task was (1) positively, to synthesize the scriptural teaching about the Father, Son, and Holy Spirit, that is, to construct an ordered account of the Trinitarian doctrine found in the Bible and ecclesiastical tradition, as well as (2) negatively, to answer objections that for God to be one and three is nonsense or a logical contradiction. Treating the Trinity after the divine unity, as Thomas does, is not the only way to organize the data of *sacra doctrina*, but it need not be taken as somehow devaluing or minimizing Trinitarian doctrine. For Thomas, the Trinity is central—the God from whom all things come and to whom they return is a communion of shared knowing and loving, a transcendent divine "friendship" beyond our powers of understanding. Organizing his account around four fundamental categories (procession, relation, person, and mission), Thomas's theology of the Trinity has remained influential in the West down to the present.

Analysis II. What Is Creation? (Ia, qq. 44–46)

Having completed his consideration of God's nature in itself, Thomas takes up God as the creator of the universe under three headings: (1) the notion of creation (qq. 44–46), (2) the kinds of creatures in God's dominion (qq. 47–102), and (3) the providence by which God governs creation (qq. 103–19).

An essential difference between the worldviews found in ancient philosophy and the belief systems of the three monotheistic faiths concerns the notion of creation. This is the difference between a view of the universe as something that always was and a quite different picture of a contingent universe brought into being by the free decision of the Creator God.[11] From the perspective of creation, God is utterly transcendent to the world, not merely its best or highest part. Aquinas's understanding of creation is a systematic expression of this foundational truth.

Thomas's treatment of the notion of creation was novel and was attacked from many sides both in his lifetime and afterward. For the "Radical Aristotelians," like Siger of Brabant, Aristotle and his commentators had rationally demonstrated that the world must be eternal; its existence in time was based on faith. To the traditional theologians who followed Augustine, such as Bonaventure, the temporal existence of the universe was not only taught by scripture, but was also a fact that could be demonstrated by reason. Thomas took his stance between both camps, thereby satisfying neither. For Aquinas, the fact of creation—the notion that the world depended absolutely on God—was a truth of faith, *but also* something demonstrable by reason. On the other hand, the duration of the universe—whether it was temporal or eternal—was something reason could not decide on its own.

Thomas's maneuvering between these opposed positions can be approached through a consideration of four Ds that help clarify his position: dependence, distinction, decision, and duration. The Christian view of "creation from nothing" (*creatio ex nihilo*) means that the world is totally *dependent* on God. It always remains, however, *distinct* from its divine source. Creation also indicates that God creates the world freely by his own *decision* and that therefore the *duration* of its existence depends on his will. God decides to make a universe marked by temporality. From the point of view of reason, however, there is nothing impossible in the idea of a universe eternally dependent on God.

In further elaborating his view of creation, Thomas employs three important distinctions. The first is that creation cannot be thought of according to the Aristotelian concept of change (*motus*), because change presupposes some underlying reality (a passive potency in Aristotle's terms), something to be changed, whereas creation has no prior something to be worked on (q. 46.2). Creation is not change; it is the beginning of a relation of absolute dependence (q. 44.1–2). The second distinction is the difference between a natural cause that has to act in a certain way (e.g., fire has to burn) and an intellectual agent, such as God, who acts on the basis of intellect and will (q. 46.1). Furthermore, as the third distinction argues, there is an essential difference between the particular intellectual agents we know and God as the universal intellectual agent, one who not only causes some condition or change, but also causes the total reality of all things in every aspect (qq. 45.2–3, 46.1). Aquinas's notion of God as the universal creative agent goes far beyond Aristotle's view of the four kinds of cause (efficient, formal, material, and final), once again revealing his analogical thinking at work.

Thomas's theology of creation is an exercise in showing how revelation can use reason while also demonstrating its limits. He draws on Aristotle's understanding of act and potency, but expands it into his own distinction between existence and essence to demonstrate that God must be absolutely different from the universe: God's essence is existence, while in all creatures there is a distinction between essence and existence. "Everything that is other than God is not its act of existence, but participates in existence" (q. 44.1). The notion of participation invoked here is crucial in showing the dependence of all things on God. Participation was not prominent in Aristotle's thought, but was a Platonic category developed by the Neoplatonist philosophers. The Neoplatonists, however, analyzed participation in terms of form; Thomas Aquinas's universe is a hierarchy of participated existences. Thus, Thomas puts together key themes from the thought of both Aristotle and Plato and his followers in crafting a theology of creation that is different from anything found in the ancient world.[12]

Thomas's treatment of the different kinds of creatures takes up almost half of the *Prima Pars* (55 of 119 questions). The reason for this extended discussion, especially about human creatures (qq. 74–102), lies in the necessity of understanding our nature and its place in the order of the universe as a way to grasp how to return to God. Here Thomas makes considerable use of Aristotle's teaching about human nature in general and the soul in particular. It would be a mistake, however, to think of this section of the *Prima Pars* as a purely philosophical treatise. It is intended to show how *sacra doctrina* can make use of the truths that reason has explored.

Thomas's anthropology has rightly attracted much attention, especially with regard to his epistemology, that is, his account of how human knowing works. It is important to remember that, for all his use of Aristotelian teaching on the soul, his teaching is fundamentally biblical, as can be seen in question 93 on humans as made in the image and likeness of God (Gen. 1:26).[13] Because God created man in his image and likeness, there is implanted in both the human intellect and will a tendency toward God as the final end, the true source of blessedness; but, since God's infinite mode of being surpasses the powers of every creature, this end can be attained only by grace, the supernatural gift by which God freely shares his own divine life. This finality is true of both the intellect's desire to attain the vision of God's essence (e.g., q. 12.4) and the will's desire toward ultimate happiness (e.g., q. 82.2).[14] Thomas's notion of the person as a dynamic intellectual being, for all its Aristotelian elements, is actually nearer to Augustine than it is to Aristotle in its emphasis on the material and historical destiny of each human.[15]

How does Thomas conceive of human knowing? Perhaps no aspect of the Dominican's thought has produced more disagreement. A few issues seem generally agreed upon; others are still contested. For Thomas, because the human intellect exists in a being that is both spiritual and material, "its proper object is an essence (*quidditas*) or nature existing in a material body" (q. 84.7). Therefore, human knowing begins in the senses and consists of a process whereby the intellect abstracts from, and eventually separates out, material sense knowing in order to gain an abstract idea, or insight, into what a thing is (*quid sit*), and then to ask whether or not this thing exists (*an sit*). Attaining truth consists in an identification of the knower and the known ("the understanding in act is the thing understood in act": q. 87.1, ad 3), as contrasted with knowing conceived of as kind of gazing on truth found in the Platonic tradition (q. 84.1). Thomas employed the analysis of knowing found in Aristotle's *On the Soul* (q. 79), especially its distinction between the intellect's natural capacity to know (the possible intellect) and the active power of questioning that empowers humans to actually arrive at knowledge (the active intellect). For Thomas, however, the active intellect, or light of knowing, is the soul's created participation in God's knowing. So while Aquinas made use of Aristotle, his epistemology goes beyond the Greek philosopher's in important ways. Following Augustine's introspective analysis of the human subject found in the *Confessions* and *On the Trinity*, Thomas attends to the act of understanding as an internal conscious operation (e.g., q. 84.7). While Thomas spends a good deal of time discussing how the concepts that answer the question "What is it?" are formed in the mind by insight, he insists that the goal of understanding is not just forming concepts about things, but the act of judging whether or not these concepts are true. Unfortunately, conceptualist accounts of Thomas's view of knowing that neglect the importance Thomas accorded to the act of judgment were to be a feature in the Thomist tradition for many centuries.

The *Secunda Pars*

The *Secunda Pars*, despite its length, has a symphonic consistency,[16] featuring as its main theme how humans move toward or away from God through habits and actions. Here Thomas draws on his view of human nature as spiritual-corporeal being as set out in the *Prima Pars* and expands on it with a meticulous study of human intentionality and action. The *Secunda Pars* opens with a brief Prologue emphasizing the connection between the first two parts of the *Summa* rooted in the notion of humans as image of God: "Because . . . man is said to be made to the image of God insofar as the image is 'an intellectual being with free choice and in control of its actions,'" declared Thomas, "it now remains to consider his image, i.e., man, insofar as he is the source of his actions, having free choice and control over his actions." Just as God freely created the universe, so too humans exercise their freedom by acting according to God's plan and making their way toward God as the goal of the universe.

The vast exercise in moral theology that follows is, once again, teleological, based on the question, "What is the purpose of human living?" Other questions that are directed to the goal of life flow from this, such as, "What are the powers and acts that humans share with animals, and what are those that are distinctive of human nature?" "What are habits and how do we distinguish between good and bad habits, that is, virtues and vices?" "What is the difference between virtues that we can gain by our own efforts and those that are God's gift?" "What is the role of the law given by God in the Old Testament and the grace made available by Christ in the New Testament?" These are some of the larger issues of the *Secunda Pars*. Embedded within them is a forest of questions and hundreds of articles. We will touch on only a handful below.

1. The *Prima Secundae*

The first five questions of the *Prima Secundae* are the key for all that comes after, because here Thomas analyzes happiness (*beatitudo*) as the goal of human freedom.[17] All the questions that follow deal with attaining that goal. For Thomas moral theology is based on the search for happiness, not on law or obligation. The Incarnation of the Word in history is the ultimate expression of the divine love that makes it possible for us to reach happiness. This locates Thomas within the tradition of what is called eudaimonistic ethics, in which moral action is determined by its relation to happiness, although there are many forms of eudaimonism.

Thomas begins by treating the ultimate end of humanity (q. 1.1–8). Properly human actions (*actus humanus*), as contrasted with those acts humans share with other animals (*actus hominis*), depend on intellect and will. Although all actions take place in view of some end or purpose, human acts are special, because they are characterized by the choice of the will concerning a goal or end, the good that the agent desires. Thomas argues that our individual choices of good outcomes, when closely analyzed, demand the existence of a single final goal, namely supreme happiness. He dismisses the usual claimants for the status of real happiness (wealth, honors, power, pleasure, etc.), things that—while good in themselves—constitute at best imperfect forms of happiness. Question 3 argues that only the uncreated Good, that is, the divine essence, can be the ultimate happiness humans strive after. As Thomas puts it, "for perfect happiness, it is necessary that the intellect attain to the very essence of the First Cause.

And thus it will have its perfection through union with God as its object, in which alone happiness is found." Although happiness consists essentially in an act of the intellect, it also involves the will insofar as the will reaches the fullness of delight when it attains the final intellectual goal. Everything that comes after this in the *Summa* exists under the sign of final beatitude—the activities that aid in the journey are good and the actions that impede it are bad.

A long analysis of human acts follows. Once again, Thomas makes use of the philosophical treatment of human action found in Aristotle, but within the perspective of the relation between nature and grace revealed in *sacra doctrina* and from the supernatural finality of the desire for the vision of God. In the prologue to question 6 he briefly introduces the rest of the *Secunda Pars*, saying that he will first treat human acts in general (IaIIae) and then move on to consider human acts in particular (IIaIIae). Concerning human acts in general, he distinguishes between the treatment of acts in themselves (qq. 6–48) and then the consideration of the principles of acts (qq. 49–114). Human acts in themselves can be further divided into acts that are distinctive of humans as possessed of intellect and rational will (qq. 6–21), and the acts that humans share with other animals, that is, the emotions, *passiones* in Latin (qq. 22–48). After treating the internal principles of acts, that is, powers and habits in questions 49–114, Thomas closes the *Prima Secundae* with two treatises once again illustrating his program of using Aristotelian thought to help understand revelation. They treat the two major extrinsic principles of human activity as directed to God: first, the instruction God gives to humans through the various forms of law, and then the supernatural gift, or grace, that provides humans with the power they need to attain the goal of the beatific vision. Here we will briefly look at what he says about grace.

Analysis III. What Is Grace? (IaIIae, 109–14)

Thomas's understanding of grace interweaves Aristotle and Augustine under the aegis of what the New Testament, especially Paul, has to say about "the surpassing grace of God that has been given to you" (2 Cor. 9:14). The Dominican took his fundamental stance about the nature and necessity of grace from Augustine, but he drew upon Aristotle's theory of human action as a form of change (*motus*), that is, a movement from possibility to actuality, to provide a deeper understanding of the action of grace in the life of the believer. Thomas also argues that grace as the participation in God has a history, so a theology of grace must treat its role in three states: (1) the time of innocence before the Fall, (2) the stage of fallen humanity, and finally (3) grace after the Incarnation.

Thomas insists that "[t]he gift of grace exceeds every faculty of created nature, since it is nothing else but a kind of participation in the divine nature that exceeds every other nature" (q. 112.1). This is why he uses the term "supernatural" more often in *Secunda Pars* than elsewhere in the *Summa,* as when he says that both Adam before the Fall and all humans afterward need a special divine help "to will and to work towards the supernatural good" (q. 109.2). Thomas's use of the term supernatural was not meant to suggest that we live in some kind of two-story universe, consisting of a natural basement and a supernatural edifice placed on top. For Thomas the universe is one, but there are two ways of conceiving of action within it: acts directed to the good proportionate to our finite created nature, and acts aimed at the final goal of human nature, the eternal vision of God (q. 109.5). The term "supernatural" provided Thomas with a way to talk about God's action in everyday human life. As he put it later in the *Tertia Pars,* "The final goal of grace is the uniting of the rational creature to God" (IIIa, q. 7.12).

The forty-four articles that make up the grace treatise deal with a number of interrelated themes. Some come from scripture and tradition, especially from Paul (as read by Augustine) on the strict necessity of grace. For Thomas, as for Augustine, grace not only was necessary for any saving action, but also was needed for the first movement toward God. Thomas's reading of Augustine also led him to the conclusion that even the person who has received grace as a habit in the soul needs further grace as an impetus to perform saving actions. To explain this, the Dominican turned to Aristotle and his view of human action in, for example, the way he employs the Philosopher's notion of habit and human operation to help understand how to talk about grace. Of particular interest in Thomas's teaching is the care with which he analyzes the relation of the divine and human wills in the process of justification by grace conceived of as both operative (i.e., God alone acts) and cooperative (i.e., where the human will has a role to play).[18] Thomas concludes his treatise on grace with a discussion of merit. If salvation depends on God's free gift, in what sense can humans be said to merit the beatific vision? Thomas answers in terms of a traditional distinction, but with a new twist. Merit, he says, can be considered in two ways: merit is truly earned (*ex condigno*) insofar as an act really deserves a reward; merit is appropriate (*ex congruo*) insofar as it is fitting for God in his generosity to reward our efforts even though they are not commensurate with the goal. Saving acts come from two sources for Thomas: from the Holy Spirit as the source of grace, in which case merit is fully earned (*ex condigno*), and from us as cooperative agents to whom God gives merit as a fitting (*ex congruo*) reward for our efforts (q. 114.3). Thomas's treatise on grace is a concise and original example of his theological method.

2. The *Secunda Secundae*

Although grace is never absent from the *Summa*, its explicit treatment at the end of the *Prima Secundae* allows Thomas to make the transition to the

Secunda Secundae where he turns from considering human acts in general to acts in particular. Here Thomas is targeting acts *insofar as they are salvific,* that is, those that proceed from grace as their primary cause, though also involving the human will as cooperating with God. His treatment here is so detailed that all but the most devoted Thomists may be excused from reading the 916 articles that constitute the *Secunda Secundae.*

Thomas begins with a Prologue, distinguishing two ways of treating moral matters (*moralia*): first, from the material in itself, as when we consider a particular virtue or vice; and second, from the perspective of different situations in life that come with their own particular moral obligations. (For example, one can treat the moral obligations that concern everyone separately from the obligations that belong to special groups.) Since virtues and vices consider the same object (e.g., chastity and lust both concern sexual activity), he considers vices along with the virtues they oppose, as well as both positive and negative commandments relating to each. Furthermore, he argues that all the virtues can ultimately be reduced to seven: the three theological virtues of faith, hope, and charity (qq. 1–46),[19] and the four cardinal virtues of prudence, justice, fortitude, and temperance (qq. 47–170). A look at his analysis of charity, the most important of the theological virtues, provides a sense of how he proceeds in this section of the *Summa.*

Analysis IV. The Virtue of Charity
(IIaIIae, qq. 23–46)

Thomas devotes twenty-four questions to charity. Perhaps the most remarkable thing about his treatment is that he places it in the category of friendship (*amicitia*), citing Jesus's words in John 15:15: "I do not call you servants any longer, but my friends" (q. 23.1).[20] Because grace perfects nature, Thomas weaves all the natural designations concerning love into his account of *caritas*, not only friendship, but also love (*amor*), delight (*delectatio*), and benevolence (*benevolentia*). They are all subsumed into this most excellent of virtues, the virtue that for Thomas is the form, or inner reality, of all the virtues.

Thomas begins with Aristotle's definition of friendship as a love of mutual benevolence founded on a sharing of goods (*Nicomachean Ethics* 8.2). Again, however, Thomas has to stretch Aristotle, because the friendship between God and humans consists in God's sharing his own blessedness, something beyond any human communication. Thomas first turns his attention to the question of charity in itself, that is, how charity is infused into the will and can be increased, diminished, or even lost. Then he considers its objects, namely, how we are to love God, our neighbor, and ourselves with God's own love. Thomas then asks what the order and the relationship of the different objects of love should be and whether it is more proper to charity to love or to be loved. For Thomas, to love belongs to charity insofar as it is charity in action; to be loved belongs to charity only in a secondary way insofar as a friend desires good for his or her friend.

Following the pattern set up for the other virtues, Thomas then turns to the effects of charity, distinguishing between internal effects (joy, peace, mercy) and external effects (beneficence, almsgiving, and fraternal correction). Next comes a long treatment of the vices opposed to charity: hate, which is opposed to delight; sloth and envy, opposed to joy; a list of vices opposed to peace (discord, contention, schism, war, quarreling, and sedition); and scandal, opposed to beneficence. Thomas argues that both love of God and love of neighbor belong to charity and that its two acts are integrally related: "The love of God is the goal to which the love of neighbor is directed" (q. 44.2–3). Just as charity is the supreme virtue, so wisdom, the highest of the gifts of the Holy Spirit, is partnered with it. Question 45 is Thomas's most expansive treatment of divine wisdom, which presupposes both faith and charity (aa. 1, 4, 5).

The treatment of the theological virtues in the first section of the *Secunda Secundae*, lengthy as it is, pales in comparison with the expanse of his discussion of the four cardinal virtues of prudence, justice, fortitude, and temperance.[21] Employing the same format in talking about them as he did with the theological virtues, Thomas asks once again, (1) what the virtue in question is in itself; (2) what are its parts, general and particular; (3) which of the gifts of the Holy Spirit correspond to it; (4) what are the opposed vices; and (5) what positive and negative precepts relate to it. Prudence, for Thomas, is the main regulating virtue, a cognitive habit that "applies universal principles to the particular conclusions of practical matters, . . . and regulates the things that relate to the goal" (q. 47.6). The virtue of justice is the subject of the longest treatise on any topic in the *Summa* (qq. 57–122). After this lengthy treatment Thomas notes (q. 123.1) that the virtues that make humans good can be impeded from following right reason in two ways: by being drawn to an object of pleasure in an irrational way, or by not following reason because of some difficulty that lies in the way. The virtue of temperance deals with the first impediment and the virtue of fortitude treats the second. Their consideration closes his monumental treatise on the virtues.

The third and last part of the *Secunda Secundae* deals with acts pertaining to particular classes of people, or associated with people in special ways (qq. 171–89). As usual in his moral theology, Thomas considers these special virtues and vices in a threefold manner. There are some activities that are based on special graces that pertain only to some people; actions that belong to particular states of life—including those associated with active and contemplative lives; and finally actions specific to the particular offices in the church.

In Thomas's time the two modes of Christian existence that had become traditional in the life of the church were allegorically figured in Martha, representing the active life of service to others, and Mary as the contemplative life of dedication to God (Luke 10). Thomas's analysis of the two lives (qq. 179–83) is among the most complete of the Middle Ages, bringing together insights from Aristotle and the teachings of the masters of Christian mystical thought, especially Augustine and Gregory the Great. His teaching is largely traditional. Although the contemplative life is higher, as a good Dominican he argued that the best life was not the purely contemplative life of the monks (q. 182.1–2), but instead the life exemplified by friars whose task it was "to hand on to others the things gained in contemplation" (*contemplata aliis tradere*: q. 188.6). Thomas never wrote a treatise on what today we would call the mystical life; this section in the *Summa* is as close as he came. The last part of this third section of the *Secunda Pars* (qq. 184–89) is ecclesiastical, presenting Thomas's view of the responsibilities of church office in its treatment of the "states of perfection," or modes of ecclesiastical life (different from the perfection of the individual).

The *Tertia Pars*

Here the topic is Christ. An in-depth treatment of Christ, we are told, "is necessary for the consummation of the whole work of theology" (*Prologus*).[22] The first part, consisting of fifty-nine questions, treats Christology explicitly in two sections: the mystery of the Incarnation (qq. 1–26) and the events of Christ's life and death (qq. 27–59).[23] The second part deals with the sacraments. Introducing this part (qq. 60–90), Thomas notes that "[a]fter the consideration of the things that belong to the mystery of the Word Incarnate, we must deal with the sacraments of the church, which have their efficacy from the Word himself." The sacraments have a Christological function in making the Redeemer's saving work available to us.

Thomas intended to finish the *Tertia Pars* with a consideration of "the happiness of eternal life to which we come by rising again through him [i.e., Christ]." Sickness and death prevented this, so his disciples, probably under the guidance of Friar Reginald, put together the *Supplement* dealing with the last four sacraments—penance (begun by Thomas), extreme unction, holy orders, and matrimony (qq. 1–68), and closing with eschatology, that is, the last events of the human pilgrimage: the resurrection of the body, the last judgment, heaven, and hell. These materials were drawn from Thomas's earlier *Writing on the Books of Sentences*.

Analysis V. The Incarnation (IIIa, qq. 1–26). Treatments of Christology are found in many of the *summae* and scholastic syntheses. These accounts tend to mix historical treatments of the events from Christ's life with theoretical considerations concerning the union of the human and divine natures in the Redeemer. The clear division between the theoretical (qq. 1–26) and the historical (qq. 27–59) sections in Thomas's Christological treatise is original, as is his wide range of sources. While the use of scripture is richer in the second section than in the first, Thomas's whole presentation is based on the truths about Christ found in *sacra doctrina*. The theological insights gained in the consideration of the union of the divine and human natures in the person of the Word provide guiding principles that help the Dominican draw out how Christ's life is both the cause of our salvation and a model for our imitation. As he says, "Every act of Christ is an instruction for us" (q. 40.1, ad 3). Thomas's Christology reveals him as a teacher, marshalling scriptural and theological authorities, principles, arguments, both deductive and fitting, to reach conclusions to deepen the reflective understanding of faith.

Christology deals with a truth that surpasses human understanding—specifically, the mystery of the Incarnation. Thomas does not attempt to uncover the secrets behind the mystery of how the divine Word took human form. Rather, his main goal is to work out a theological grammar that shows which expressions of the meaning of the Incarnation are coherent with faith and which are erroneous or heretical. Incarnation was a free act of God, as was Christ's choice to die on the cross. Therefore, the foundations of Christology are not in necessary reasons or arguments. Much of what is contained here is argument from what Thomas calls *convenientia*, that is, showing the "fittingness" of God's action in history. Of course, there are also some strictly deductive arguments that can be made from principles held by faith. The interplay between the various modes of argument in Thomas's Christology is one of its distinctive features.

Thomas had already treated the Incarnation at length in Book 3 of his *Writing on the Sentences* and in the *Summa contra Gentiles* IV.27–55. This may account for the fact that few of the topics treated in questions 1 to 26 are new (only 14 articles out of 151). Still, on several issues the treatment of the Incarnation in the *Tertia Pars* is original. The first question deals with the fittingness of the Incarnation. Article 3 asks whether the Word would have become incarnate even if Adam had not sinned. Various scholastic teachers had answered this question in different ways, and there was a tradition of cosmic Christology, arguing on the basis of passages in John and Paul that the perfection of the universe made it fitting that God should become man even in the absence of human sin. Others followed Augustine in saying that the scriptures teach that the Incarnation took place in order to repair the damage caused by Adam's sin. In the *Writing on the Sentences* and the *Summa contra Gentiles* Thomas held that either view was possible. Here he argues that "it is more fittingly said that the work of the Incarnation was ordained by God as a remedy for sin, so that had sin not existed there would not have been an Incarnation." As ever, Thomas sticks close to scripture. He was convinced that the biblical passages about Christ's primacy deal with final causality only, that is, they teach about the fittingness of the Incarnation in relation to the return of sinful humanity to its goal, not about a Christology implicit in creation itself. Others, such as Duns Scotus, disagreed.

Questions 2 to 6 investigate what the union of God and man in Christ actually is (*quid sit*). The union cannot take place in either the divine or human nature as such (otherwise one nature would be changed into the other), so it must take place in the person (Greek: *hypostasis*) of the Word (q. 2.2). In technical terms, it is a "hypostatic union." A person, understood as "an individual substance of a rational nature," possesses a nature but is distinct from it (e.g., we do not say "John is humanity," but "John is a man"). Therefore, says Aquinas, "If human nature is not united to the Word of God in the person, it is not united at all and faith in the Incarnation is totally removed and the whole Christian faith is uprooted." The hypostatic union involves a special kind of grace, the grace of union which Thomas defines as "the personal existence itself that is freely and divinely given to human nature in the person of the Word and is the term of the act of assumption." Thomas makes a distinction between "union," which signifies the fact that Christ is both God and man, and "assumption," which is the action by which the Person of the Word takes up human nature into himself (q. 6.6).

In considering knowledge as one of the perfections of Christ, Thomas differentiates Christ's different kinds of knowledge: his divine knowledge, his beatific knowledge, the knowledge infused in him by the gift of the Holy Spirit, and finally that which he acquired by the exercise of his human intellect (q. 9.4, and the whole of q. 12). Even before the Resurrection, Thomas insists that Christ had the special privilege of existing both as a *comprehensor*, one who possessed the vision of God, and as a *viator*, one who existed as a human learner. Thomas holds that on the human level Christ advanced in knowledge with regard to both intellectual habits and acts of knowing (q. 12.2), thus paying more attention to Christ's acquired knowledge than other scholastics did. The final perfection that Thomas investigates is Christ's "power," that is, the range of his ability to act (q. 13). He shows that as a human being, Christ had to respect certain limits to his power—God alone is truly omnipotent. Christ had real human emotions (*passiones*), such as physical pain, sadness, fear, wonder, and anger (q. 15.5–9). While Thomas qualifies the extent to which Christ possessed these human emotions more than theologians would today, this section of his Christology was original in its time.

The first twenty-six questions of the *Tertia Pars* are among the most sustained accounts of Christology in all of scholastic theology, but Thomas decided that even this was not enough, so he crafted a treatment of the "deeds and sufferings" (*acta et passa*) of Christ's life, death, resurrection, and exaltation in questions 27 to 59. Though often neglected, this detailed and existential treatment of Christ's life is original and important. Thomas divided it into four parts: Christ's entry into the world (qq. 27–39), the course of Christ's life (qq. 40–45), Christ's exit from the world (his death on the cross; qq. 41–52), and finally his exaltation after this life (qq. 53–59). Here Thomas draws extensively on the patristic authors, especially their biblical commentaries. Especially impressive is the way Thomas develops the theology of Christ's work of redemption, coordinating the notion of satisfaction for sin with other biblical motifs, such as reconciliation, merit, sacrifice, obedience, and especially love, the primary motivation for our salvation. At the end of his massive treatment of Christology, Thomas concludes in a typically laconic way, "Enough for now about the mystery of the Incarnation" (q. 59.6, ad 3).

After finishing the Christological treatise, in question 60 Thomas turns to a consideration of the sacraments.[24] He divides the section into a treatment of *sacramentum* in general (qq. 60–65) and a consideration of what by his time had become the doctrine of the seven specific sacraments of the church (qq. 66–90). The understanding of "sacrament" underwent a shift in the twelfth century, away from a broad notion of sacrament as the full range of rituals and practices used in Christian life toward a carefully defined concept of seven rites ordained by Christ and handed on by the apostles as the means by which Christ and his grace become present to believers. Thomas had considered the sacraments in his two previous syntheses, but there are new accents in his treatment in the *Summa*. The scholastics had inherited two understandings of the term *sacramentum*—Augustine's stress on sacrament as a "sacred sign," and Isidore of Seville's notion of a "sacred secret." By the time of Peter Lombard (d. 1160), the Augustinian notion of the sacred sign had prevailed, but with a growing emphasis on the idea that the seven "true sacraments" were signs that *caused* grace. This concern with causality was not just an academic conceit; it was an attempt to do justice to Paul and John's depiction of the power inherent in baptism and the Eucharist. But how can a sign be a cause? And how are the divine and human agents related in the administration of the sacraments? What is the difference between the "sacramental" signs of the Old Testament, especially circumcision, and the sacraments of the New Testament? Why and how do some sacraments, such as baptism and holy orders, effect a permanent change in the recipient so that they are not to be repeated, while others, such as penance and the reception of the Eucharist, are repeatable? These and other questions led Thomas to devote considerable attention to this aspect of *sacra doctrina*.

Thomas places the notion of sacrament "in the category of sign" in question 60.1, before providing his specific understanding in article 2: "A sacrament is a sign of a sacred thing insofar as it sanctifies people."

The Christological core of Thomas's teaching is set forth in article 3 where he discusses the triple signification of sacrament as including (1) the effective cause of our sanctification, namely, Christ's Passion understood as the whole Paschal mystery; (2) the form (formal cause) of our sanctification, that is, the grace of Christ and the Holy Spirit and the virtues attendant upon it; and (3) the final cause, namely, eternal life. A sacrament, therefore, is a unique kind of causal sign that is simultaneously commemorative of the past, demonstrative of what is taking place in the present, and prognostic of the future. The acts of worship that constitute the sacraments as saving signs require the use of both a material element (e.g., washing with water in baptism) and verbal formulas, the words of faith that express the meaning of the action (q. 60.4–8). After investigating the necessity of the sacraments, Thomas takes up the question of how the sacraments function as causes of grace in question 62. In questions 27 to 59 Thomas showed how Christ's human nature functioned as an instrumental cause of our salvation insofar as this human nature was joined to the person of the Word (i.e., an *attached* instrument). In question 62 he extends this insight by arguing that the sacraments are *detached* instrumental causes of salvation: "And therefore, the sacraments of the New Law are at one and the same time a cause and a sign. Hence, as is commonly said, 'They bring about what they signify'" (62.1, ad 1; and a. 5).[25] Question 63 considers the nature of the permanent effect (*character*) of the sacraments, which is the reason why some sacraments can only be received once. This, as Thomas explains, is because the character is a deputation that enables the recipient to take a specific role in Christian worship. Question 64 takes up the respective roles of God, Christ, and the human minister in administering the sacraments in terms of the distinction between God's originating causality and the instrumental causality of the human minister. Finally, question 65 shows why it was fitting that Christ instituted seven sacraments. In Thomas's understanding of the sacramental system there is both a movement from above by which God in Christ brings down saving grace to humanity, and a movement upward in the church's worship of its God and Savior, so that, in Liam Walsh's words, "[the sacraments] allow God to act humanly in signs made by humans."[26]

Having established the nature, efficacy, and number of the sacraments, Thomas proceeds with his investigation of each sacrament, beginning with baptism (qq. 66–71), proceeding to confirmation (q. 72), and moving on to the Eucharist (qq. 73–83), which he argues is the most important sacrament (q. 65.3). Thomas finally took up the sacrament of penance, which was always much discussed in scholastic literature. He managed to write only seven questions (qq. 84–90) before the incident of December 6, 1273.

Conclusion

Thomas's death left his students and colleagues with the vast but unfinished *Summa theologiae*. The work was already circulating in some of its separate parts, and there is no question that the world of scholastic theology—not just the Dominicans—was eager to examine the book. But Thomas's views, at least in some areas, were controversial. What was to become of his great effort to provide a sapiential ordering to the whole of *sacra doctrina*?

The Tides of Thomism, 1275–1850

The influence of the thought of Thomas Aquinas in the more than seven centuries since his death is not just a question of the reception of the *Summa theologiae*, although reading and commentating on the *Summa* has been central to the story of Thomism (the word *Thomismus* appears as early as the fourteenth century). It would also be a mistake to restrict the story of the *Summa* only to those who are usually identified as Thomists (*Thomistae*). Some of the most significant moments in the history of the reception of the book concern readers who either attacked the work, misunderstood it (sometimes creatively),[1] or used it for their own purposes. Limiting the biography of the *Summa* to the history of the Thomist Schools would miss what is often most interesting about the reception of the book, the encounters between the *Summa* and non-Thomist thinkers. This chapter will look at a variety of Thomisms, but also consider some of these encounters. To try to include them all would be to write a history of Western theology and philosophy over the past seven hundred years.

Even trying to write the history of Thomism itself is so difficult a task that no attempt at a general account has been made for more than a century and a half.[2] Over a thousand commentaries on the *Summa theologiae*, in whole or in part, exist,[3] and one catalogue of Thomists lists 2,034 names.[4] What does it take to become a Thomist? Is it enough to self-consciously proclaim oneself as a follower of St. Thomas? Or does one also have to adhere to a number of key principles or teachings of Thomas, especially as identified by those who argue for a distinction between what they call "classical," or "strict," Thomism, and a broad, or eclectic, use of aspects of Thomas along with other systems of thought?[5] Any list of the key principles of Thomism is a product of interpretation, so we should not be surprised that these lists have varied greatly over the centuries. Strict constructionist positions on what constitutes Thomism have a number of drawbacks. The first is the paradox that although Thomas was a theologian who used philosophy, many forms of strict Thomism, such as Neothomism, have been primarily philosophical in nature. It is also true that although Thomas strove to be clear about the relation of faith and reason, his works have been read over the centuries in quite different ways, giving rise to at least two main views of the respective roles of theology and philosophy: one that sees philosophy as being pursued primarily within the context of the work of theology, the other viewpoint arguing that philosophy is a separate discipline for Thomism.[6] A second difficulty is the sheer multiplicity of views claimed as Thomist over the centuries, a diversity that has not lessened in the past hundred years. A generation ago Henri de Lubac remarked, "As for the 'Thomism' of our own century, I have too often found in it a system that is too rigid and yet at the same time not faithful enough to the Doctor it claims as its authority. I have also seen it raised too often (in complete good faith) like a pavilion to cover the most diverse merchandise to be able to take it seriously."[7] Surveying the history of Thomism down to the seventeenth century, the English Dominican Gerald Vann was no less pessimistic: "In the main . . . the history of Thomism during these centuries is a history of failure; and a failure precisely . . . to meet the intellectual needs of the times."[8] To use Aquinas's own language, Thomism is at best an analogical term; perhaps an equivocal one. Nonetheless, even equivocations have histories.

The First Half-Century (1274–1325)

The period from Thomas's death to his canonization was formative for much that followed. A few general observations will help for introducing this period. First of all, Thomas failed in his objective of having the *Summa* replace the unwieldy *Sentences* of Peter Lombard, even among the Dominicans.[9]

The Lombard's book was too solidly entrenched in the theological curriculum to yield its place, in part because it was used as a jumping-off place for individual theological speculation. In an era when tensions and divisions among theological camps were growing, different schools and masters could use the Lombard's text for their own purposes far more easily than they could the carefully structured and closely argued *Summa*. A second point concerns the paradox of Thomas's position in the scholastic world during these fifty years. Thomas left no successor, or formal "school." Shortly after his death he was attacked both by ecclesiastical authority and by theological opponents among the Neo-Augustinian thinkers, primarily Franciscans, but also including the secular master Henry of Ghent (d. 1293). The Dominicans sprang to his defense. These attacks testify to Thomas's importance: one does not have to man the walls of theological correctness against a nonentity. Although it would take two centuries before the *Summa* would become the textbook that Thomas had intended, its influence was major, as we can see both from the number of manuscripts that survive and the ways in which the book was used, especially in moral theology and in speculation on God.

Thomas's road to fame was a bumpy one. The condemnation of the Radical Aristotelians in 1270 does not appear to have put a halt to their suspect teaching in the Arts Faculty at Paris. The Neo-Augustinian theologians, the heirs of Bonaventure, were exasperated by the Aristotelian positions advanced by some Parisian philosophers, such as their claims for the eternity of the universe. Their anger, however, was also directed against Thomas, who they felt had given away too much to Aristotle, especially on such issues as the substantial unity of the human soul and the philosophical demonstrability of the creation of the universe in time. While many of the specific issues under dispute were philosophical, important theological questions were also at stake: In what sense is theology a science? What are the limits of the use of philosophy in the work of theology? The disputes came to a head in 1277 with dual condemnations by the bishops of Paris and Oxford of lists of erroneous teachings, which included a number shared by Thomas.[10]

All medievalists see these condemnations as significant. For Etienne Gilson and his followers they were not so much a cause as a symptom of the desire to rein in "the excessive philosophical independence of some masters in philosophy and theology"—a defensive move that signified the end of the "golden age" of scholasticism.[11] Thomas's way of building a bridge between theology and philosophy was under attack by theologians who deplored what has been called "Greco-Arabian Necessitarianism," that is, philosophical arguments that seemed to limit God's freedom of action. These views, which Thomas would also have rejected, are expressed in a number of the condemned articles; for example, "God would not have been able to make prime matter without the help of a celestial body" (art. 38; see also arts. 43–44). Other scholars have seen the condemnations as a reaction to the birth pangs of a new form of independent philosophical teaching,[12] which Bishop Stephen Tempier wanted to get under control by subordinating philosophy to theology.[13] The meaning and effect of the events of 1277 continue to be disputed. It seems clear, however, that the condemnations shifted the ground in the theological world, at least in Paris, and they certainly were a challenge to Thomas's life's work.

Although much has been written about the condemnations, there are still puzzling issues.[14] In Paris Bishop Tempier, former chancellor of the university, established a commission of masters (including the anti-Thomist Henry of Ghent) to investigate dangerous teaching in the Arts Faculty. On March 7, 1277, he issued a condemnation of 219 propositions with attendant excommunication for anyone holding them. The preface to the document explicitly attacks "some Parisian students in the Arts who have gone beyond the limits of their own Faculty and who have dared to treat and dispute in class . . . some open and detestable errors, or rather vanities and false ravings." The list is a mixture of propositions in no order, some of them contradictory. The articles are mostly philosophical, including many from Aristotle and Averroes, though they also contain errors about theology—"Nothing is to be believed unless it is known in itself or can be derived from things known in themselves" (art. 37); "No one knows anything more by knowing theology" (art. 153). Although there is some dispute about the actual number, about sixteen articles involve Thomas's teaching, especially on such issues as the nature of separate substances (i.e., angels), individuation by matter, and the operation of the intellect. Thomas's controversial doctrine of the unicity of form in humanity, however, is not mentioned. The probable reason why it is not found is that during the same month of March Tempier instituted two theological commissions, one against the Augustinian theologian, Giles of Rome (d. 1316), a former student of Thomas, and the other against the deceased Dominican himself. On March 28, fifty-one propositions from Giles were condemned, including his teaching on the unicity of form, and he was denied his license to teach. The second commission singled out as erroneous Thomas's view "That in man there is only one substantial form, that is, the intellectual soul" (Ia, q. 76.4), but for reasons still unclear,[15] Tempier did not issue a condemnation, but forwarded the material to Rome where it was still under discussion in 1284. Nothing ever happened with this process.

A parallel case evolved in Oxford, the center of theology in England. On March 18, 1277, Robert Kilwardby, archbishop of Canterbury and himself a former Dominican and master at Oxford, issued a document prohibiting the teaching (not formally condemning) thirty errors in grammar, logic, and natural philosophy. The twelfth of the errors in natural philosophy was unicity of form: "[It is an error to say] that the vegetative, sensitive and intellective principles are one simple form." It is commonly said that this and a number of the other prohibited errors in natural philosophy were directed at Thomas, but he is not mentioned by name and these issues were under discussion in many circles.

The attacks against Thomas continued, but they moved into the realm of the tensions between the two mendicant orders, with a concerted Franciscan push against the Dominican theologian. About 1279 the English Franciscan William de la Mare, who had succeeded Thomas's adversary John Pecham in the Franciscan chair of theology at Paris, published a *Correctory of Brother Thomas*, listing 117 passages from Aquinas's writings, mostly from the first two parts of the *Summa theologiae*, with "corrections" based on Augustine and Bonaventure. This work was approved by the Franciscan General Chapter of Strassburg of 1282, which commanded that only "intelligent readers" could use Thomas's *Summa*—and only in tandem with William's corrections.

Notwithstanding the episcopal actions in Paris and Oxford, the Dominicans came to Thomas's defense by issuing a number of directives in their General Chapters. For example, the 1279 Chapter of Paris issued a general ban against "irreverent or unbecoming talk about Thomas and his writings."[16]

Another Paris Chapter (1286) legislated that all Dominicans should study, promote, and defend "the doctrine of the late venerable master, Friar Thomas Aquinas," a regulation reiterated at Saragossa in 1309. The Chapter of Metz in 1313 issued an order forbidding any friar from teaching something contrary to "what is commonly held as the opinion" of Thomas, a reference to the French Dominican Durandus of St. Pourçain (ca. 1270–1334), whose commentary on the *Sentences* adopted many positions against Thomas. At the behest of the Dominican Master General a commission drew up a list of Durandus's anti-Thomist errors in 1314. (After several years of controversy, Durandus escaped the power of the order by being named Bishop of Limoux in 1317.) Some Dominican Chapters issued positive commands concerning Thomas, as when the 1315 Chapter of Bologna ordered that all the houses of general studies should acquire "a complete set of the writings of Friar Thomas, especially in theology."

William's *Correctory* was a serious threat to Thomas's heritage, so the next decade saw five Dominican responses, or *Correctories of the Correction* (or *Corruption*, as the Dominicans called it). These are traditionally seen as expressions of the first "Thomistic School."[17] The respondents were international (English, French, Italian), and they were not "masters," but younger friars who sprang to the defense of the great Dominican *magister*.[18] A study of their works indicates that they generally had a good sense of many of Thomas's controversial teachings, such as the distinction of essence and existence, the philosophical neutrality of the duration of creation, and the unicity of the substantial form of the human person. The core of the dispute, however, was the relation between faith and reason and the role of philosophical reasoning in theology.[19] Some of the "correctors" suffered for their adherence to Thomas. Richard Knapwell, who began his teaching at Oxford in 1284, soon ran afoul of Thomas's old adversary, the intransigent Franciscan John Pecham, who had become archbishop of Canterbury in 1279. The archbishop, who had renewed his predecessor Kilwardby's restrictions on erroneous teaching, condemned Knapwell as a heretic in 1286 and excommunicated him, largely over the issue of unicity of form. Knapwell appealed to Rome, but when he arrived there he found a Franciscan pope, Nicholas IV, who forbade him to teach. He died not long after.

The *Correctory* literature provides us with a sense of what was at stake in the arguments between Franciscans and Dominicans, but they were the tip of the even larger iceberg of the growing influence of the *Summa*. Dominican legislation encouraged reading Thomas and the *Summa*, and, even though the Lombard's *Sentences* remained the standard text, the Dominican chapters insisted that it be read with the help of material taken from the *Summa*. Thomas had strong (though not universal) support across the Dominican network of houses throughout Europe.

Some Dominican theologians, such as John of Freiburg, composed moral handbooks that excerpted and simplified the IIaIIae of the *Summa* for the use of confessors, and therefore had a real effect on the lives of the laity.[20] Thomas was also widely read outside the Dominican Order, if not always correctly. The Augustinian Giles of Rome, who got into difficulty for some of his Thomist views, seems to have been the first to introduce a serious misunderstanding of Thomas's teaching on the distinction of existence (*esse*) and essence (*essentia*) in created beings, conceiving of them as two things (*res*) and not as principles of created things. This misunderstanding was to mislead Thomists for centuries. Another sign of the popularity of Thomas's *Summa* was the widespread copying and dissemination of the work in the fifty years following his death.[21]

A brief look at two encounters of the *Summa* with major scholastics of this first half century can suggest the work's role in the wider intellectual arena. The Franciscan John Duns Scotus (ca. 1266–1308), like Thomas, had a short but productive career.[22] "The Subtle Doctor" was not only an original thinker, but also an influential one. Various Scotist Schools were active for centuries. Scotus was especially concerned with the scholastics of his era, such as Henry of Ghent and Godfrey of Fontaines, but he knew the writings of Bonaventure and of Thomas, including the *Summa*. Like Thomas, his writings were mined both for philosophy and for theology, and he contrasts with the Dominican on issues in both respects. For example, Thomas had argued that all our language about God is analogical, but Scotus held that when we talk about God as the perfect being, the language we use of God and creatures must be univocal if we are to attain real knowledge of God. Hence, Scotus was also far less apophatic, or negative, in his theology, because "being" has a generic conceptual sense that gives us some positive idea of God (for Aquinas *esse* is not a concept). In anthropology Scotus was a voluntarist, insisting (against Thomas) that the will is autonomous, not linked to the direction of the intellect. Similar contrasts show up regarding many theological doctrines, as in Scotus's arguments for the Immaculate Conception of Mary, or in his defense of the doctrine that the Word would have become flesh even if Adam had not sinned. As an example, we can look at the differences between the two scholastics on the nature of theology itself.

Scotus's teaching on *theologia* or *doctrina revelata* (i.e., revealed teaching) seems to have developed over the course of his career, so it is not always easy to pin down his position.[23] The lengthy Prologue to his *Ordinatio* forms a parallel to Thomas's treatment of *sacra doctrina* in question 1 of the *Prima Pars*, treated in chapter 2.[24] Another, perhaps more mature, treatment, is found in the *Reportatio Parisiensia* (book III, d. 24).[25] A major difference that emerges from these texts is that Scotus treats theology as a *habitus* in the mind of the theologian, rather than primarily as a process of teaching and learning as did Aquinas. In the *Ordinatio* Scotus's consideration, more detailed than Thomas's, deals with five issues: (1) the necessity of revealed teaching, (2) the sufficiency of scripture, (3) the object of theology, (4) theology as a science, and (5) theology as a practical science. In discussing the first question, "Whether another teaching [besides philosophy] that is supernaturally inspired is necessary for a human person in this life," Scotus shows awareness of the Paris condemnation of 1277 and the threat of a philosophy that claims to be sufficient for humans to reach the goal of life. He begins by contrasting the arguments of the philosophers that reason alone is sufficient for human happiness with the arguments of the theologians that revealed teaching is necessary for salvation (Thomas is explicitly cited in one place).[26] Scotus disagrees with the theologians, however, because he contends that God could, on the basis of his absolute freedom, save someone who does not have the gift of faith (Prol., Pars 1, q. unica, nn. 54–56). The Franciscan does not side with the philosophers either, because he holds that natural reason on its own cannot solve the dilemma of whether or not the enjoyment of God is our end; revelation teaches us that it is.

Scotus also differs from Thomas when it comes to the scientific character of theology. In refuting Thomas in book III, d. 24 (nn. 16, 22) of the *Reportatio Parisiensia* he denies that in the strict Aristotelian sense we can have both science and faith about the same thing in the same respect, but at the beginning of the work, in his "Prologue," questions 1 to 3, he argues that theology as "a science of faith" possesses a scientific character insofar as it orders its contents "under the proper aspect of deity," although its forms of evidence will not be the same as those of other sciences.[27] Scotus also differs from Thomas, who argued that *sacra doctrina/theologia* was primarily theoretical and to a lesser extent practical, by insisting that theology is only a practical science related to right action, that is, to loving God. This is true even with regard to the teachings that seem theoretical, such as the statement "God is a Trinity." No, says Scotus: "I say that such truths are practical; theology includes in a virtual way knowledge of the correctness of the love tending towards the three persons, so that if an act were elicited towards one person alone and excluding the others, it would not be a correct act" (*Ordinatio*, Prol. Pars 5, q. 1, n. 322).

The German Dominican Meister Eckhart (ca. 1260–1328), like Thomas, was also twice called to the Dominican chair at Paris. Eckhart was a famous vernacular preacher and mystic, but also a profound philosopher-theologian, who planned a massive, but incomplete, synthesis he called the *Three-Part Work* (*Opus tripartitum*). The first part of this work, the *Work of Propositions*, was intended to be an exercise in axiomatic theology; but the second, the *Work of Questions*, was to have been modeled on Thomas's *Summa*. Most of what survives is from the third part, the *Work of Expositions*, consisting of commentaries on the Bible designed to aid in preaching. Eckhart had a profound respect for Thomas and appealed to the example of his confrere, now a saint, when he himself was under investigation for heresy at the end of his life (1326–28). Eckhart knew Thomas and the *Summa* inside out, citing it hundreds of times in his Latin writings and showing a special preference for the *Prima Pars*.[28] Nevertheless, Eckhart was not a strict follower of Thomas. Rather, he used Thomas as a conversation partner in creating his own system of thought.

Eckhart's independence can be partly explained by the reception of Thomas and the *Summa* among the German Dominicans trained at the *studium generale* in Cologne. The German Dominican School, especially its contributions to philosophy, has come in for considerable study in recent years. Between about 1260 and 1350 the German Dominicans produced a succession of thinkers whose philosophical and theological positions, though often influenced by Thomas, show real independence.[29] Albert the Great's turn to the negative theology of Dionysius, as well as developments of his Aristotelian theory of the intellect with marked Neoplatonic and Avicennan elements, shaped many of these thinkers in ways that have not yet been fully studied. Eckhart's contemporary, Dietrich of Freiburg (ca. 1250–1320), who has emerged as the most interesting philosophical mind among the German friars, took a decidedly anti-Thomist stance on many issues, including his introduction of the notion of "conceptual being" and his teaching on the relation of the active intellect and natural felicity. Other Dominicans, such as John of Sterngassen (active ca. 1320), were Thomist in outlook. Meister Eckhart was independent.

Eckhart was influenced by Dietrich, but his thought differed from his contemporary's as much as it did from Thomas's.[30] Citing a few examples of the differences between Thomas and Eckhart will illustrate the German's independent use of Thomas. First, Eckhart, unlike Thomas, held that a priori proofs for God's existence were valid. Second, with regard to the perfective terms used of God, in his *Parisian Questions* given in Paris 1302–3 Eckhart parts company with Thomas on the priority of the language of existence (*esse*) when used of God. "I declare," he says, "it is not my present opinion that God understands because he exists, but rather that he exists because he understands. God is intellect and understanding and his understanding is the ground of his existence" (*Parisian Questions*, q. 1). Third, Eckhart's understanding of the nature of the intellect is different from that of Thomas. While Thomas held that the human mind is made "to the image" of God (Ia, q. 92), Eckhart insisted that the human mind was both made *to the image* (hence, different from God) and, on a deeper level, identically *one with the image*, or Second Person of the Trinity. This helps explain why, fourth, Eckhart's view of human action is nonteleological (not goal-oriented), in distinction from Thomas's view that human moral action is always directed to final happiness. For Eckhart, since the intellect is identical with God's image, human virtuous activity, like God's, should be "without a why," that is, done for itself alone, not for any further purpose. Good action springs from the inner divine formal cause, the ground of the soul, not from striving toward an external final cause (e.g., *Commentary on John* n. 336).[31]

At the root of Eckhart's creative misreading of Thomas is a contrasting notion of the relation of theology and philosophy. Aquinas distinguished between truths known by reason and those taught only by faith and sought to show the relation, as well as the nonopposition of philosophy and theology. For Eckhart reason and revelation are coterminous, differing not in what they teach, but only in the way they teach. In a noted passage he says, "Moses [i.e., the Old Testament], Christ, and the Philosopher [Aristotle] teach the same thing, differing only in the way they teach, namely as worthy of belief [Moses], as probable or likely [Aristotle], and as truth" (*Commentary on John* n. 185). Aquinas contended that there could be no real contradiction between the truths taught by faith and human reason; for Eckhart human reason as the presence of God in the mind is capable of knowing and unknowing both natural truths and the mysteries of faith, such as the Trinity. Given his insistence on the perfect reciprocity between reason and revelation, he describes his scriptural commentaries as designed "to show how the truths of natural principles, conclusions and properties are well intimated for him 'who has ears to hear' [Matt. 13:43] in the very words of sacred scripture that are interpreted through these natural truths" (*Commentary on John* n. 3). For Eckhart, in contrast to Thomas, all metaphysical, ethical, and theological truths are fundamentally one.

Thomas Aquinas's position in the church changed dramatically in the second decade of the fourteenth century. Pope John XXII ascended the throne of Peter in 1316. His fondness for Aquinas is evident both from his own library and from the support he gave to the Dominican initiation of a canonization inquiry regarding the teacher who was already being called the "common doctor" (*doctor communis*). After inquiries held at Naples and Fossanova in 1319 and 1321, the case went to the pope at Avignon and on July 18, 1323, John solemnly proclaimed Thomas Aquinas a saint in strong language: "He has illuminated the church more than all the other doctors. In his books a person can gain more profit in a year than in the teaching of others for a whole lifetime." The canonization process also involved a theological component, because John XXII commissioned the Dominican Giovanni Dominici (d. 1324) to compile a long abbreviation of the *Summa*, which in effect was something like a commentary, the first of its kind. After all the controversy surrounding his teaching, Thomas had achieved a recognition that put him beyond condemnation. Under pressure from the Paris masters, on February 14, 1325, Stephen Bourret, the bishop of Paris, revoked Tempier's condemnation of 1277, insofar as it might affect Thomas. The wheel had turned.

The Fortunes of the *Summa* (1325–1500)

The next two centuries reveal a shifting story in the fortunes of the *Summa theologiae*. The fourteenth-century world of academic theology was divided into contending schools of Scotists, Albertists, Thomists, and especially the "modernists" (*moderni*), or "Nominalists," who adopted in greater or less degree the critical philosophy and theology of William of Ockham (d. 1347), as contrasted to the "old-timers" (*antiqui*), or the "Realists," who adhered to the teaching of one or the other of the major thirteenth-century scholastics. Thomas Aquinas was the official theologian of the Dominicans, but this did not make his *Summa* their main teaching text. Nevertheless, Thomas's book was recognized as an impressive summary of the teaching of the Latin Church, as is evident from the fact that it was translated into Armenian and Greek in the fourteenth century, as well as into Middle High German.

Byzantine interest in Thomas is noteworthy, given the opposition between Orthodox theology and the Latin West. Nevertheless, there was a line of fourteenth- and fifteenth-century Greek theologians, some of them converts to Catholicism, who studied and translated Thomas's works, including Demetrios Cydones (d. 1397), who rendered both the *Summa theologiae* and the *Summa contra Gentiles* into Greek. Byzantine Thomism was primarily philosophical and not theological: Thomas was seen as the best interpreter of Aristotle.[32] Greek interest in Thomas continued on into the fifteenth century, as can be seen in Cardinal Bessarion (d. 1472), whose thought was shaped by Orthodox theology, but who read Thomas assiduously both before and after his conversion to Rome.[33] There were even translations of parts of the *Summa* into Hebrew. The interest of Jewish philosophers in the thought of Thomas as a way to counter Averroistic readings of Aristotle that conflicted with the Hebrew Bible, something that had begun in the late thirteenth century with thinkers like Rabbi Hillel of Verona and Jehudah ben Daniel Romano, continued on during the fourteenth century.[34] Still, the fourteenth century in general did not witness the appearance of major Thomists or original uses of the *Summa*, perhaps due to the crisis of society and academia at the time of the Black Death in the middle of the century.

The early fifteenth century marked a change in the fortunes of Thomas and the *Summa theologiae*. Three important developments deserve attention. The first was a renewed focus on the *Summa* accompanied by the growth of the commentarial tradition.

The second was the encounter of Thomas's thought and the *Summa* with Humanism in Italy. The third factor was the birth of printing and the possibilities it provided for the dissemination of the book to a wider audience.

As Bernard Lonergan once observed, "St. Thomas practiced a method, the method of the *quaestio*. The great Thomists practiced a method, the method of the commentary."[35] It was in the fifteenth century that the *Summa* began to become the subject of multiple commentaries. The commentary, according to Paul Griffiths, is a form of "meta-work" based on another text and featuring (1) extensive quotation, summary, or paraphrase of the base text, that (2) quantitatively or qualitatively outweighs other elements in the work, and that (3) provides the structure and order of the meta-work.[36] With the exception of the Bible, few books in the history of Christianity have inspired more commentaries than the *Summa*. For the succession of schools of Thomism teaching and commenting on the book became the essential mortar. Thomist commentators often invoked general interpretive principles. Two of the most common were reading "according to the mind of St. Thomas" (*ad mentem S. Thomae*), and speaking of "St. Thomas as his own interpreter" (*Divus Thomas sui interpres*)—certainly laudable principles, although they did little to curtail the variety of readings.

The earliest of the great commentators was the French Dominican John Capreolus (1380–1444), who taught at Paris and Toulouse. Called "the Leader of the Thomists," Capreolus was a defender of Thomas's views against other scholastics, such as Henry of Ghent, Durandus of St. Pourçain, Scotus, and William of Ockham. He did so through a massive commentary on Thomas's *Writing on the Sentences* called the *Defenses of the Theology of St. Thomas*, written between 1408 and 1433. The *Defenses* do, however, contain much material from the *Summa*. Capreolus begins his work with the pious statement dear to all Thomist commentators: "I make one prefatory remark, namely that through this whole reading I have one supposition and it is that I intend to introduce nothing of my own, but only the views that seem to me to belong to the mind of St. Thomas, and I will not employ any proofs or conclusions beyond his own words, except on rare occasions."[37] With Capreolus, however, we can detect a major shift from Thomas's view of theology as *sacra doctrina*. For Thomas sacred teaching is scientific because it is primarily a form of deductive teaching (i.e., an activity) based on revealed first principles. For Capreolus theology is a science of conclusions: "It is not a science of the articles of faith, but of the conclusions which follow from them."[38] Many later Thomist commentators were to follow Capreolus to the extent that they treated faith as a kind of preliminary starting point, so that theology became a form of natural metaphysical argumentation.[39] This misunderstanding was instrumental in the development

　　　　　　　　　　　　　　　　　　CHAPTER 4

of the tradition of seeing Thomas as more of a philosopher than a theologian.

During the fifteenth century, first in Germany and soon spreading widely, both Dominicans and non-Dominicans began to employ the *Summa* as a school text. The University of Cologne was the earliest center of teaching and commenting on the *Summa*.[40] The initiators were secular priests. The Dutch Henry of Gorcum (called "the Monarch of the Cologne Thomists") studied at Paris, came to Cologne to teach in 1420, and died in 1431. It is not known if his *Compendium of the Summa theologiae*, printed in 1473, is actually based on class lectures, but it is one of the first major commentaries. His disciple, the Belgian secular master John Tinctor (d. 1469), wrote a *Commentary on the Summa theologiae* in the 1460s that was certainly based on class lectures. John's commentary concentrated on the objections and doubts raised about Thomas's positions, so he does not deal much with the actual arguments in the body of the *Summa* articles. Quite different was the contemporary work of the Dominican Gerard of Elten (d. 1484), the *Lectura on the First Part of the Summa of St. Thomas*. Gerard, one of the first to reflect on the structure of the *Summa*, divided his treatment of each of Thomas's articles into a "declaration of the text," where he reduced the arguments in the body of the articles into syllogisms, and a "solution of difficulties," in which he added his own reflections. Perhaps the most important of the Cologne Thomists was another Dominican, Konrad Köllin, whose *Exposition of the IaIIae of the Angelic Doctor St. Thomas Aquinas* was published in 1512 on the eve of the Reformation. By this time the teaching of the *Summa* was widespread in Germany (e.g., Vienna, Freiburg, Rostock) and was also found in other countries. The Italian Dominican Tomasso di Vio (1469–1534), called "Cajetan," began to lecture on the *Summa* in Pavia in 1497, and the Belgian Dominican, Peter Crockaert, began to teach the *Summa* in Paris in 1507. The spreading use of Thomas's work in the fifteenth century is also evident in the creation of tools to assist in using the book, such as abbreviations, concordances, indices (this process had begun in the fourteenth century). The prolific Dutch scholar Denys the Carthusian (d. 1471) produced a compendium to the *Summa* called the *Summa of Orthodox Faith*, while the Italian Dominican Peter of Bergamo (d. 1482) compiled the massive index known as the *Golden Table* (*Tabula aurea*), first printed in 1473. This work, often appended to editions of the *Summa* even into modern times, was the most complete index until the publication of the forty-nine volume electronically generated *Index Thomisticus* by Robert Busa (1974–81).

The role of Thomas and the *Summa theologiae* in Renaissance Humanism, especially in Italy, has often been misunderstood.[41] Disputes about the meaning of the Renaissance have been many, at least since the publication of the Swiss historian Jacob Burkhardt's

The Renaissance in 1864. Burkhardt stressed the break between the Humanist intellectuals and artists who turned back to the Classical past to devote themselves to the *studia humanitatis*, on the one hand, and, on the other, their scholastic predecessors of what the Humanists themselves were the first to call "the Middle Age." Later investigators, however, pointed out that many of the figures considered central to the Renaissance, for all their criticisms of the narrow scholasticism and rigid clerical ecclesiasticalism of their day, were religious reformers who were familiar, though in varying ways, with the thought of the scholastics, not least Thomas Aquinas. Humanist emphasis on Platonic theology by no means led to a total break with scholasticism and Thomas.

A number of Italian Dominicans, such as Vincent Bandelli of Castronovo (1435–1506), were able to combine devotion to Thomas and his *Summa* with Humanist sympathies, although members of other religious orders sought to resist the growing movement to elevate Thomas above other doctrinal authorities. Thus, the Carmelite Battista Spagnoli, called "Mantuanus" (1447–1516), wrote a treatise around 1490 called *The Golden Work Against the Thomists* in which he argued that Thomas was a worthy member of the third class of teachers (the scholastics), but these were inferior in authority to the first class (the apostles) and even the second class (the Fathers of the patristic period). Thomas would not have disagreed. Renaissance emphasis on the power of rhetoric fostered the preaching of sermons in praise of Thomas on his feast day of March 7.[42] The most interesting was given by the layman Lorenzo Valla in Rome at the church of Santa Maria sopra Minerva in 1457, the year of his death. Valla's antipanegyric praises Thomas's sanctity, but has less use for his scholasticism, because the Dominican, like other scholastics, mixed the water of philosophy with the wine of sacred teaching. Thomas's thought was also used in the Philosophical Faculty at the University of Padua in the fifteenth and early sixteenth centuries, when his views were seen as a counter to the reigning Averroistic interpretation of Aristotle.[43]

Interesting encounters of Thomas with Renaissance thought are found in the premier Platonizing philosophers of the Renaissance, Marsilio Ficino (d. 1499) and Giovanni Pico della Mirandola (d. 1494). Neither can be considered a Thomist, but they both knew the friar's works. Ficino's *Platonic Theology Concerning the Immortality of the Soul*, composed between 1469 and 1474, was the closest thing to a *summa* produced by the Renaissance philosophers. Ficino found an ally in Thomas for his attempt to demonstrate the immortality of the soul against the Averroists. He occasionally cites Thomas by name and silently refers to him in a number of places. Ficino, however, uses Thomas within the context of his own Neoplatonizing philosophy. For example, in the discussion of the divine nature in book 2, Ficino makes use of Thomas about twenty-five times and includes a reference to "our divine Thomas, the splendor of theology" (II.12.8). Ficino's program, however, remains fundamentally Platonic. Ficino makes use primarily of the *Summa contra Gentiles* not the *Summa theologiae*.[44] Giovanni Pico della Mirandola read widely, not only in ancient philosophy, Jewish and Arabic sources, but also among the scholastics. His bold syncretistic plan to dispute nine hundred theses at Rome was stopped by Innocent VIII, who condemned thirteen of the announced theses as dangerous or heretical in 1487. Among the list of nine hundred were forty-five of Thomist origin (mostly from the *Writing on the Sentences*).[45]

Finally, the fifteenth century saw the invention of printing, a development that made a radical change in the accessibility of texts to the reading public. A sign of the importance of the *Summa* is that it was printed early and often. If the Gutenberg Bible can be dated to circa 1455, it is noteworthy that by circa 1463 the earliest printing of the most popular part of the *Summa*, the IIaIIae, appeared in Strassburg. The *Prima Pars* was printed in Venice in 1484, and both the Ia and the IaIIae came out together in Basel in the same year. (Given that manuscripts of the *Summa* generally were copied as parts, this practice is not surprising.) The first complete printing of the *Summa theologiae* also appeared in Basel in 1485. Altogether there were twenty-nine incunables, or early printings, of the *Summa* before 1501. It was no accident that the same half century that saw the emergence of the *Summa* as a class text witnessed the work's rapid movement into print.

The *Summa* in Divided Christianity (1500–1650)

By the first quarter of the sixteenth century the *Summa* was widely used in teaching theology. The European religious scene, however, shifted dramatically after 1517, when the Augustinian Martin Luther mounted a challenge to the whole edifice of scholastic theology and the medieval conception of the church. Before looking at the encounter between Thomas and Luther, it will be useful to consider the status of the *Summa* among Catholic theologians during the period 1500–1550. In Roman Catholicism the sixteenth and seventeenth centuries are often described as the "Golden Age" of Thomist commentators, the time of "Second Thomism."[46] Many theologians set forth their views about philosophy, theology, ethics, and politics as much through their commentaries on the thirteenth-century Dominican's book as through their own writings. Still, we should not think that everyone was a Thomist. As in the late Middle Ages, different theological schools still contended, but Thomism acquired a preponderance it had not enjoyed previously.

The most significant figure in early sixteenth-century Thomism was Tommaso di Vio, Cardinal Cajetan.[47] Cajetan was educated in Naples and

Bologna and in the 1490s began lecturing at Padua, where he contended with but also absorbed some of the Averroistic Aristotelianism popular in this center of Italian philosophy. He then went to Pavia (1497–99), where he was the first Italian to teach the *Summa*. The friar taught at Rome (1501–8) before becoming the Master General of the Dominicans (1508–18). Deeply involved in the Roman reaction against Luther, Cajetan confronted the Reformer at the Diet of Augsburg in 1518, served on the theological commission that resulted in Luther's excommunication in 1520, and wrote a number of treatises against his teaching. Cajetan became a bishop, papal legate, and eventually a cardinal. This Italian Dominican was not only a skilled politician but also an original thinker who wrote extensively on philosophy (especially commentaries on Aristotle), on biblical exegesis (late in life), and on Thomas. In the 1490s he composed a series of treatises collected under the title *The Analogy of Names* (1498) in which he advanced a metaphysics of analogy that he claimed was an explanation of Thomas, but which recent scholarship has seen as more his own construction. Nevertheless, *The Analogy of Names* was one of the most influential texts in the history of Thomism. Cajetan also took up the monumental task of writing the first full commentary on the *Summa theologiae*, which he published between 1508 and 1522. Although he expressed a basic adherence to Thomas, Cajetan was not loath to disagree with his Dominican predecessor on such issues as the ability of reason to prove the soul's immortality, which the cardinal denied. Cajetan's view of sacred teaching as a "habit of conclusions" was also not that of Thomas. Cajetan was not the first to introduce the non-Thomist notion of "pure nature" (*natura pura*) into his reading of the *Summa*'s account of the creation and finality of human nature, but he was surely among the most influential.[48] The significant differences between the two thinkers, however, cannot be explored here.

Cajetan's commentary on the *Summa* is based on a distinction between "formal exposition," where he explains Thomas's arguments in syllogistic form, and a "magisterial exposition," where he treats issues raised by Aquinas's positions. His respect for his predecessor is evident in the words of the Preface:

> In the case of such a great collection of issues our vast Thomas (*immensus Thomas*) is not less to be admired for how he brought arguments and words together in a rational way than in how he treated and penetrated such a mass of material. The limpidity of his style is such that nothing can be added to it; taking anything away would be to reduce it to ashes.

Cajetan was one of the most influential of all Thomists, as witnessed by the fact that both the first papally approved printing of the *Summa* issued by Pius V in 1570–71 as well as the edition sponsored by Leo XIII include Cajetan's *Commentary* along with the text of Thomas. Cajetan's contemporary

Francisco Silvestri of Ferrara (d. 1528), who also served as Dominican Master General, wrote an equally classic *Commentary on the Summa contra Gentiles* during this same period.

Cajetan's Thomism, while the most significant of its time, had many rivals, as the influence of the Second Thomism deepened its hold on Catholic Europe. In the period up to the opening of the Council of Trent in 1545 and Luther's death in 1546, Thomism, and especially lecturing on the *Summa theologiae*, spread widely. If the use of the *Summa* had begun in Germany and moved on to Italy and France, its penetration into Spain, which became the most powerful Catholic state in the mid-sixteenth century, was crucial. As noted above, Peter Crockaert taught the *Summa* at Paris from 1507. Among his pupils was the Spanish Dominican Francisco de Vitoria (ca. 1483–1546), who studied at Paris between 1508 and 1522 and then returned to Spain to teach first at Valladolid (1523–26) and then at Salamanca (1526–46), the premier Spanish theological faculty. In both places Vitoria introduced the custom of lecturing on the *Summa* and thus helped establish the hold that Thomas had on Spanish theology for more than a century. Vitoria's most noted contribution to Thomism was his *Commentary on the Secunda Secundae*, which laid the foundation for his defense of the human rights of the Indians of the New World and for his famous writings on just war (1538, 1539). The Dominican's work has been seen as at the origins of modern views on international law and had an influence on the Protestant jurist and theologian Hugo Grotius (d. 1645). Other Salamancan Dominicans who left commentaries on the *Summa* include Vitoria's pupil Domingo de Soto (d. 1560).[49]

Thomists of the first half of the sixteenth century were in the forefront of the fight against Luther and his followers. But what was Luther's view of Thomas and the *Summa*? Did the Reformer have a real encounter with the book? Luther was trained in medieval scholastic theology at Erfurt, though not in the *via Thomae* but in the *via moderna* of the Nominalists. He was certainly aware of Thomas to some extent through the use of the Dominican by the Nominalist theologian Gabriel Biel (d. 1495). Luther may have read something of Thomas during his training and after he began teaching at Wittenberg in 1511, but we are not sure. Thomism did not play any real role in his intellectual formation.

During the second decade of the sixteenth century Luther broke with the scholasticism in which he had been trained and eventually with the papal church. Luther's initial reaction was primarily directed against the Nominalistic theology he knew well, as can be seen in his *Disputation Against Scholastic Theology* of 1517. Like some Humanists but for different reasons, Luther felt that the original sin of scholasticism was the introduction of the foul water of philosophy, especially that of Aristotle, into the limpid springs of the Gospel. Thomas was certainly more than tainted by this error, so, however much

Luther did or did not know of the Dominican, there was a significant difference in their conceptions of theology.

Luther had harsh things to say about Thomas from 1518 on. In his 1524 treatise *Against the New Idol* he denounces Thomas "as the source and foundation of all heresy, error, and obliteration of the Gospel."[50] Luther's sharp language against Thomas, however, was provoked not so much by Thomas as by his followers.[51] The Reformer's main opponents in his attack on the validity of indulgences and other religious abuses of the day were Dominican Thomists, like Cajetan, Sylvester Prierias (d. 1523), and Ambrose Catharinus (d. 1553). Against their claims for Thomas as the ultimate authority in theology, Luther argued that no teacher, let alone Thomas, has an authority higher than scripture and the councils. Thomas's views were theological opinions, not defined truth as the Thomists contended. As the disputes deepened, Luther came to agree with his opponents that Thomas's teaching was, indeed, the mainstay of the papal church and was therefore in opposition to the Bible. In *The Babylonian Captivity of the Church* of October 1520, he even denounces "the Thomistic church."[52] If Luther decisively rejected the authoritative Thomism of his day, we can still ask about the deeper relation between the theology of the Reformer and that of the thirteenth-century Dominican.

Modern research has given a more nuanced answer to this question than what was common in the pre-ecumenical era. Work still needs to be done on how much Luther may have actually had direct knowledge of Thomas and the *Summa*—though the answer seems to be relatively little.[53] If historical research does not yield strong connections, attempts to compare the mode of theology of Aquinas and Luther, such as those conducted by Otto Hermann Pesch, have been more fruitful.[54] The details of these comparisons cannot be pursued here, but the core of Pesch's argument is that for all their serious differences, Thomas and Luther were often not as far apart as has been thought in the past, especially on such questions as the certitude of salvation, sin and grace, the role of faith and charity in salvation, and saving knowledge of God. Pesch argues that Thomas's "sapiential style" of theology, that is, looking at the world objectively from God's point of view as it were, in contrast to Luther's "experiential style," that is, "a way of doing theology from within the self-actuation of our existence in faith,"[55] always needs to be taken into account when seeking to determine how far the Reformer really disagrees with the author of the *Summa theologiae*.

Had Luther been the only person disaffected by the abuses and intransigence of the late medieval church, he would have remained a footnote. His call for reexamination of questionable teachings and practices met with rapid success, not only among theologians, but also in wide swaths of believers across Europe. The Reformation sundering of Western Christianity was a matter of both ecclesiastical structures and theological differences, though the latter have often come to be seen today as misunderstandings as much as real differences. Obviously, Thomas and his *Summa theologiae* were mostly viewed in negative terms by the majority of the Reformers and their successors, but the rise of what has been called "Protestant scholasticism" in the late sixteenth century represents a complicated adoption and rejection of medieval scholasticism in general and of Thomas in particular. Learned Protestant divines, both on the Continent and in England, could scarcely avoid Thomas and the *Summa*, though their degree of knowledge and use varied.[56]

During the two decades of upheaval that followed Luther's attack on the papacy, the popes continued to resist serious reform while more and more areas in Europe abandoned obedience to Rome. Eventually, in December 1545 a council convened by Paul III met in Trent to address both the doctrinal challenges of the Reformers and to take up the issue of the reform of Catholic Christianity. The Council of Trent that met sporadically between 1545 and 1563 addressed the first charge by clearly laying out Roman Catholic theology against Reformation views on such issues as the relation of the Bible and tradition, original sin, justification, and the sacraments. Reform decrees on the parochial and diocesan levels were approved, but not for the Roman curia, where Pius IV, the last pope of the council period, reserved such reforms to himself. The Council of Trent helped form modern Catholicism down to the mid-twentieth century— the First Vatican Council of 1870 can be considered as a kind of addendum to issues of ecclesiology that Trent postponed due to lack of consensus.[57]

A popular legend (one repeated by Leo XIII) has it that Thomas's *Summa theologiae* was set up on the altar at Trent next to the Bible so that the council fathers could pay equal homage to these joint sources of truth. This never happened. The shifting membership of Trent during its many sessions included representatives from all the late medieval schools of theology: Thomists (i.e., Dominicans), Scotists (Franciscans, who appear to have had the largest number), and Augustinians, whose major representative was Cardinal Seripando (d. 1563). With regard to dogmatic issues, the council fathers wisely abstained from making decisions favoring one or the other position in the contested world of late medieval theology. As "committee documents," the Tridentine decrees were framed in ways that would exclude Protestant "error," but allow for readings consonant with Dominican, Franciscan, or Augustinian interpretations. A study of the conflicts between Thomists and Scotists in the debates on such issues as justification and the causality of the sacraments shows how consensus language was gradually achieved.[58] Later attempts to make Trent a "Thomist" rejection of the Reformation are wide of the mark.[59] This is not to say that the Thomists who attended Trent, such as

Melchior Cano (d. 1560), Domingo de Soto, and Pietro Bertano, did not play significant roles in the discussions and final decisions.

The growing role of Thomism in Roman Catholicism was a product not of Trent, but of the classroom and of the papacy. Along with the widening academic use of the *Summa theologiae* in the first half of the sixteenth century, the proliferation of editions and commentaries grew exponentially. The Council of Trent and the subsequent Counter-Reformation introduced the period often referred to as the time of Baroque scholasticism (ca. 1550–1700). The Dominican Order, especially in Spain, emerged as the center of Thomism through the efforts of classic commentators on the *Summa* like Bartolomeo de Medina (d. 1580) and Domingo Bañez (d. 1604), as well as Seraphino Capponi (d. 1614) in Italy. Bañez, who served as Teresa of Avila's confessor, was praised by Etienne Gilson as one of the few commentators on the *Summa* who got Thomas's teaching on the primacy of existence (*esse*) right. Commenting on Ia, question 3.4, Bañez put it with some exasperation: "And this is what Thomas calls out so often and what Thomists don't want to hear, that existence is the actuality of every form and nature."[60] Nonetheless, the most significant boost to the role of Thomas and the *Summa* in the wake of Trent was the initiative of the stern Dominican Michael Ghislieri, Pope Pius V (1566–72), who did much to further the reform initiated at Trent. In 1567 Pius took the unprecedented step of naming Thomas Aquinas a "Doctor of the Church," a title hitherto restricted to eight traditional patristic teachers (four from Eastern Christianity and four from Western). Pius also sponsored what was meant to be the definitive edition of *Opera omnia* of Thomas Aquinas, which appeared in seventeen volumes in Rome in 1570–71 (the *Editio Piana*). The emergence of Thomas and the *Summa* as the central theological resource for Catholicism was now an established fact.

Another key moment in the history of Thomism was the adoption of the "Angelic Doctor" (as he was now called) as the official teacher of the Jesuit order organized by Ignatius Loyola from the 1520s on and given papal recognition in 1540. Ignatius himself (1491–1556) was not a theologian, but a converted soldier and courtier who devoted his energy, organizing skills, and deep piety to creating a new form of religious life that would combine action and contemplation. The highly disciplined, centralized, and well-educated Jesuits became the mainstay of the Counter-Reformation. Ignatius's preference for the theology of Thomas Aquinas was evident (see his *Constitutions of the Jesuit Order* 4.14.1), but it was not until 1593 that the Jesuit General Chapter adopted Thomas as their official theologian. This decree, however, did allow departure from Thomas's views in extraordinary cases, an exception that the Jesuits seem to have employed too frequently—at least as viewed by the Dominicans. The Jesuit theological school in Rome, the *Collegio Romano*, founded by Ignatius in 1551 and later supported by Pope Gregory XIII (1572–85)—today named after him as the Gregorian University—became another center for the study of Thomas. The Jesuits produced their own commentators on the *Summa*, such as Francisco de Toledo (d. 1596) and Gabriel Vazquez (d. 1604). The Jesuits were also responsible for the earliest dissemination of Thomas into Asia, when seventeenth-century Jesuit missionaries led by Louis Buglio produced an edited Chinese version of the *Summa* (1654–78).[61]

The greatest of the Jesuit thinkers of the time was Francisco Suarez (1548–1617). Suarez was very familiar with Thomas and wrote a long commentary on the *Summa* published between 1590 and 1620. This commentary was unusual in paying particular attention to the Christology of Thomas's *Tertia Pars*, to which the Jesuit devoted no fewer than three volumes. A glance at these reveals how complex commentaries on the *Summa* had become. For example, the first volume of Suarez's commentary on the IIIa, covering questions 1 to 26 (published 1590), contains not only Thomas's text and Suarez's explanation of it, but no fewer than fifty-six disputations, some of considerable length, defending and extending Thomas's views. Suarez, like Cajetan, was an independent thinker, philosophically and theologically. The Spanish Jesuit's metaphysics, for example, broke with Thomas and came closer to Scotus in teaching that being is a general category embracing both God and creatures and in denying the distinction of essence and existence in created beings.[62] Despite his distance from Thomas, Suarezian "Thomism" was formative in Jesuit education for centuries.

During this time the Dominicans and Jesuits entered into theological combat, debates that often involved differing interpretations of Thomas. The most notorious was the controversy over the relation of grace and freedom called the "*De auxiliis* Controversy" because it concerned the "aids" (*auxilia*) to divine grace. This quarrel disturbed Catholicism from the 1580s until 1611 and continued to poison relations between the two orders well into the twentieth century. In 1584 Domingo Bañez published a *Treatise on the System of Physical Predestination Founded on Preexistent Divine Decrees* in which he set forth, on the basis of texts from Thomas, a form of predestination centered on divine decrees giving "irresistible grace" by way of what he called "physical premotion" to some people and denying it to others. Many thought that Bañez's view denied the role of human freedom in the path to salvation. In 1588 the Jesuit Luis de Molina (d. 1600) argued for another approach in his *Concord of Free Choice with the Gifts of Grace, Divine Foreknowledge, Providence, Predestination and Reprobation*. Molina contended that human cooperation with grace can be guaranteed only by grounding the efficacy of grace not in a divine decree, but in God's foreknowledge of free human actions through what he called "middle knowledge" (*scientia media*), that is, the knowledge God alone has of what humans would do in any set of circumstances.[63] Therefore, God gives grace to those he foreknows will cooperate with it. Bañez and the Dominicans said that they were following the authority of Augustine and Aquinas and accused Molina and his Jesuit supporters of Pelagianism. The Jesuits, including their foremost theologian Robert Bellarmine (d. 1621), responded that they were not innovators and that Bañez's view contradicted Trent and was not different from that of the Protestant predestinarian theologian John Calvin. Disputations were held, accusations hurled back and forth, pamphlets and treatises issued on all sides. In 1598 Clement VIII mandated silence on both groups and established a special "Congregation on the Aids" to investigate the question. Molina came close to being condemned in 1598 and 1601, but the Jesuits staved off defeat. Clement VIII and his successor Paul V reserved final judgment to the papacy and heard endless arguments that resulted in mounds of evidence. Although the majority of the consulters wanted to censure some of Molina's propositions, many of the cardinals and higher clergy convinced the pope that the issues involved were too intricate for a decision at the time. No conclusion was ever reached. The Congregation on the Aids was dissolved, and in 1607 Pope Paul issued an injunction ordering both parties to stop calling each other heretics and "hoping that they abstain from mutual harsh words signifying bitterness of soul." On December 11, 1611, the Inquisition issued a decree that all writings on grace, even under the pretext of commenting on St. Thomas, would henceforth require its examination and approbation.

The last of the great Thomist commentators of this Golden Age began his teaching shortly afterward. John Poinsot, the son of a Hungarian nobleman and a Portuguese mother, was born in 1589 and entered the Dominicans in 1612, taking the religious name John of St. Thomas. He started teaching in 1620 and spent most of his career at the University of Alcalà, dying in 1644. John moved in the highest ecclesiastical and political circles, serving as advisor and confessor of Philip IV of Spain. He published his *Thomistic Philosophical Course* between 1632 and 1636, a work that remained in use in Catholic seminaries down into the twentieth century, though often in abridged or adapted form. His greatest work, however, was the unfinished eight-volume *Thomistic Theological Course* (1620–44), which followed the order of the *Summa*, although with many digressions and discussions of current issues. John of St. Thomas made extensive use of earlier commentaries, especially Cajetan and Suarez, though often disagreeing with the Jesuit. The most famous part of his influential commentary (the last section he lived to complete) was his treatise on the seven gifts of the Holy Spirit discussed in *Summa theologiae* IaIIae, question 68, and IIaIIae, questions 8–9, 19, 45, 52, 121, and 139.[64]

The Decline of Thomism (1650–1850)

The authority of Aquinas and the *Summa* in early modern Catholicism was evident not just in the ongoing loyalty of the Dominicans and the adherence of the Jesuits, but also by the fact that perhaps the greatest school of Thomists of the 1600s was that of the Spanish Carmelites. A succession of Carmelite professors at Alcalà called the *Complutenses* wrote a seven-volume philosophical survey of Thomas's thought published from 1624 on. An even more weighty *Theological Course on the Summa of St. Thomas* was put out by the Carmelites of Salamanca between 1600 and 1725.[65] The work of these *Salmanticenses*, as they were called, one of the largest commentaries on the *Summa*, is a monument to how different ages have understood and (mis)understood the *Summa*. These Carmelite commentators, for example, did not even deign to discuss the first two questions of the *Prima Pars* in which Thomas explains the significance of *sacra doctrina* and the existence of God, issues that were to become major in twentieth-century Thomism. The volumes devoted to the *Tertia Pars* feature an extensive treatment of the first twenty-six questions on Christology and then go on to treat the sacraments, but totally neglect questions 27 to 59 on Christ's saving mysteries.

By the time the *Salmanticenses* completed their immense—and skewed—commentarial efforts Thomism was no longer an important part of the cutting edge of philosophical discussion in Europe. René Descartes published his *Discourse on Method* in 1637 and his *Meditations on First Philosophy* appeared in 1641. Although Descartes had some knowledge of scholastic thinking, his books set philosophy on a new course in their quest for a new form of philosophical certitude and the construction of a carefully articulated mathematical model for metaphysics. The Enlightenment philosophers who followed him, such as John Locke, David Hume, Christian Wolff, and Immanuel Kant, had little sympathy with Thomas, even when they had some familiarity with his thought. Comparative analyses of the philosophical differences between Aquinas and Kant, as well as other eighteenth- and nineteenth-century philosophers, have been written, but these Thomist encounters are too complicated to be addressed here. The distance between Thomas's *sacra doctrina* based on revealed truth and Kant's critical and ethical philosophy is well illustrated by the title of one of Kant's most famous writings, *Religion within the Limits of Reason Alone* (1793).

In the eighteenth and early nineteenth centuries what Thomism there was in Catholic universities and seminaries was restricted to the production of long, dry commentaries. There was a good deal of eclecticism in many Catholic schools, with philosophical textbooks often more based on Suarez, Descartes, or Wolff, than on Thomas.[66] Many Catholics of the Enlightenment Era lost interest in the world of Thomist commentary, concentrating rather on the positive, historical theology that had been born in the seventeenth century and grew strong in the eighteenth, as can be seen in the editions and publications of the Benedictines of the Congregation of St. Maur and the Bollandist Jesuits who inaugurated the critical edition of the lives of the saints (the *Acta Sanctorum*).

Despite this shift in interest, Thomism did not die out between 1700 and 1850, although even devoted Thomists admit that this era can be described as the nadir of Thomism. An incident from the end of the period illustrating the decline can be found in the career of the most famous Catholic thinker of the nineteenth century, John Henry Newman (1801–90). After Newman converted to Catholicism in 1846, he went to Rome for a year (November 1846–June 1847) to prepare for being ordained a Catholic priest. Newman had just published one of his most profound works, the *Essay on the Development of Christian Doctrine*. Already equipped with a deep knowledge of patristic theology, Newman seems to have hoped to find out more about Thomas Aquinas at the center of Catholicism. He was disappointed. A Jesuit father he encountered told him, "O no—he said—Aristotle is in no favor here—no, not in Rome: nor St. Thomas. I have read Aristotle and St. Thomas, and owe a great deal to them, but they are out of favor here and throughout Italy. St. Thomas is a great saint—people don't dare to speak against him—they profess to reverence him, but put him aside."[67] Newman's love of the Fathers had drawn him to Rome, but his knowledge of Thomas remained a distant and notional one, not a real knowing. Things were about to change.

The Rise and Fall of Neothomism

CHAPTER 5

The Origins of Neothomism

Neothomism is the name given to the papally supported form of Thomism that developed in the second half of the nineteenth century The movement needs to be seen as a political event as much as it was an intellectual one.[1] The triumph of Enlightenment philosophy and its claim that theology should be based on reason restricted what Thomism there was in the eighteenth and early nineteenth centuries to the intellectual ghetto of Catholic schools and seminaries. Political support for this world, however, remained strong until the French Revolution and Napoleon's meteoric career overturned the Old Regime and convulsed Europe for a quarter century (1789–1815). The reestablishment of something like the old political system at the Congress of Vienna of 1815 was a setback to the forces unleashed by the Revolution, one that resulted in the nineteenth-century struggles between revolutionary-reformist trends on the one hand and monarchical-restorationist resistance on the other. Pius VII (pope 1800–23), who had been imprisoned and browbeaten by Napoleon, played a role at Vienna and set an example for most of the nineteenth-century popes of a restorationist agenda, both politically and intellectually. Papal resistance to representative government, political liberalism, and the trappings of modernity (even the railroad) was strong under Pius's successors, Leo XII, Pius VIII, and Gregory XVI. Giovanni Maria Mastai-Ferretti, elected Pope Pius IX in 1846, had a reputation for favoring liberal ideas. In 1848, however, Pius had to flee Rome amid a popular revolution. When he returned in 1850 with the aid of a French army sent by Napoleon III, he turned against liberal ideas, such as representative government, freedom of conscience, and a free press.

The struggle between modernity and what was seen as tradition was also evident in philosophy and theology.[2] There were many issues under debate, but the relation between faith and reason was the nodal point. To what extent can the truths of faith be open to rational investigation, and on the basis of what kind of reasoning? What epistemology and theological method can best lead to a theology that will answer the Enlightenment critique of traditional Christianity? In the first half of the nineteenth century some Catholic thinkers, especially in Germany, turned to Critical, Romantic, and Idealist philosophies to try to present a coherent understanding of the relation of faith and reason for the modern era. Perhaps the most daring were the Catholic theologians at Tübingen, such as J. S. von Drey, J. A. Mohler, and J. E. Kuhn. Another influential figure in this camp was the priest Georg Hermes (1775–1831), who sought to reconcile Catholic theology with Kant's critical philosophy. Hermes was posthumously condemned in 1835. Such condemnations were rather rare in the first half of the nineteenth century, perhaps because while the Roman authorities could agree on particular errors and what they deemed false approaches, they had as yet no systematic exposition of philosophical and theological truth to serve as a standard for judging error on a large scale. This is where Neothomism stepped into the picture.[3]

The triumph of Neothomism was rapid, but, like most revolutions in thought, it had a significant, if hidden, period of gestation.[4] The Dominicans played an important role, especially when the order was revived after the upheavals of the Revolution and Napoleonic period. Dominican houses in Spain and Italy (especially Rome and Naples) became centers of the teaching of Thomas. Also important for the return to the Angelic Doctor was the Collegio Alberoni in Piacenza, run by Vincentian priests. The Jesuit order as a whole was not sympathetic to Aquinas in the first half of the nineteenth century. Under pressure from unfriendly rulers, Clement XIV had suppressed the order in 1773, but it was restored by a decree of Pius VII in 1814. The Jesuit university in Rome, the Collegio Romano, was given back to the order in 1824. Among its first students was Count Vincenzo Gioacchino Pecci (1810–1903), later elected pope Leo XIII in 1878. The first rector was Luigi Taparelli d'Azeglio (1793–1862), a fervent student of Thomas Aquinas. D'Azeglio, however, met with resistance against Thomas by Jesuit professors wedded to Suarez and Descartes, so he had to resort to teaching Aquinas secretly to a group of enthusiastic students. Young Pecci seems to have found his love for Thomas while at the Collegio, for as early as 1828 he wrote home to ask for a copy of the *Summa theologiae* which he knew to be in the family library at Carpineto. In 1829 d'Azeglio was banished from Rome to the Jesuit house in Naples.

Pius IX's agenda after his return to Rome was dedicated to constructing a "fortress Catholicism" against the political and intellectual threats of the modern world. In 1864 he issued his "Syllabus of Errors," a list of eighty theses or pronouncements already condemned in other papal documents. Grouped under ten headings, these errors included pantheism, naturalism, rationalism, indifferentism, socialism, communism, and liberalism, as well as various errors on the church's relation to civil society, marriage, and the temporal power of the papacy. (A number of the more extreme of these condemnations were reversed in the documents of Vatican II.) Pius's main accomplishment, however, was the First Vatican Council of 1869–70, which issued two important documents defining truths central to the positions adopted in the Syllabus. The Constitution *Pastor Aeternus* affirmed the pope's primacy of jurisdiction in the church, and, more important, defined his infallibility in matters of faith and morals, while a second Constitution, *Dei Filius*, defined the relationship between faith and reason in a way basically consistent with Thomas's view as found in the *Summa*, though with less emphasis than Thomas on the radically apophatic nature of knowledge of God. The generally Neoscholastic and Neothomist tone of the document is not surprising. The original schema for the constitution was drawn up by the Jesuit J. B. Franzelin, who was not a member of the Jesuit Neothomists, but when this schema proved unwieldy, it was revised by Bishop Martin of Paderborn with the assistance of his classmate, the German Jesuit Johannes Kleutgen (1811–83). Kleutgen, known as "Thomas reborn" (*Thomas redivivus*), was to become an influential figure of the first generation of Neothomism.[5]

The Neothomist wave grew in importance in the 1870s, not only in Rome, but throughout Europe in Spain, Paris, Louvain, and Vienna. Dominicans, such as the Spaniard Zeferino Gonzales and the Italian Tommaso Zigliara, were significant figures. In order to coalesce into a real force, however, central institutional support was necessary. This came with the accession of Gioacchino Pecci to the chair of

Peter. Leo XIII remains a difficult figure to interpret. His social encyclicals, his condemnation of slavery, his opening the Vatican archives to research, and his outreach to some forms of democratic government witness a shift away from the intransigence of Pius IX. But Leo was scarcely a liberal. He had been closely involved with the drafting of the "Syllabus of Errors," and his wholehearted embrace of Neothomism was designed to create a systematic, militant, and uncompromising bulwark against modern thought. To quote James Hennessy, "What he wanted was to realize ultramontane goals unrealized under Pius IX by intellectualizing the combat with modernity. . . . He would not come to terms with the modern values; rather, he would restore in the world an objective and immutable order, with the church as its most effective guardian."[6] Neothomism was Leo's agent for this ambitious program, which was fundamentally a response to the philosophical and theological errors of the Enlightenment and post-Enlightenment world. Leo's program, however, also had a positive component, because he hoped that a renewed Thomism would serve as an integrating force both in the intellectual and social realms. Despite its eventual collapse, Neothomism was one of the most important initiatives of modern Catholicism and is central to the story of the *Summa theologiae*.

Pope Leo moved quickly to make Neothomism the official teaching of Catholicism, taking no hostages among its opponents. In the year of his election he brought the Jesuits of the Collegio Romano to heel by demanding that Thomism become the main form of instruction and appointing Kleutgen as the Dean of Faculty. For all his adherence to Thomism, however, Kleutgen was primarily a historical theologian, and it was not until 1885 that Louis Billot (1846–1931), a future cardinal, was appointed to teach Thomistic philosophy. (Of Billot it has been said, "History and its methods were beyond his horizon.")[7] In the meantime, the pope, his brother Joseph, and the Jesuit Thomist Matteo Liberatore (with the possible assistance of Kleutgen) had composed the "Magna Carta" of Neothomism, the Encyclical *Aeterni Patris*, issued on August 4, 1879. As the most important document in the history of the official reception of the *Summa theologiae*, the encyclical demands careful attention.

As an authoritative teaching document (though not infallible in the sense defined in Vatican I), *Aeterni Patris* sets out a theoretical argument and provides mandates, if in a general way, for the steps needed to realize this ideal. Unlike earlier conciliar and papal documents stretching back into antiquity dealing with particular theological questions, such as the approval by the Council of Ephesus (431 C.E.) of Cyril of Alexandria's teaching on Christ against that of Nestorius, *Aeterni Patris* gives its support to a whole system of thought, Neoscholastic philosophy, as the foundation for a theology that would strike the correct balance between reason and faith. The long-standing emphasis on Thomas as a philosopher, evident in many of the classic commentators, thus became enshrined in papal teaching. Leo and his advisors intended *Aeterni Patris* as a response to the strong rationalism of much Enlightenment philosophy: in order to meet a new kind of total challenge, an equally total response was needed on the part of the revived, centralized, and now infallible, papacy.

Addressed to the bishops of the Catholic Church, *Aeterni Patris* lays out an argument for the Pauline view of the superiority of Christian wisdom over the false wisdom of the world, provides a sketch (quite ahistorical) of the development of Christian philosophy, argues for Thomas Aquinas as the supreme form of scholastic philosophy, and calls upon the Catholic world, especially its educators, to return to the teaching of Thomas as "the invincible bulwark of faith" (para. 24). Leo's case is based on a conviction of the inherent unity of the "solid doctrine of the Fathers and the scholastics, who so clearly and forcibly demonstrate the firm foundations of the faith, ... and its perfect concord with reason" (para. 27). Although many patristic authors are mentioned in paragraphs 3 to 13, aside from brief references to Bonaventure and Albert the Great, Thomas represents the scholastic philosophy that Leo holds out as the ideal for Christian education. The argument given is primarily based on authority and tradition—Thomas has been recognized as the supreme doctor by all the best teachers, the religious orders, the universities, and the popes and councils (paras. 14–23). Revived Thomism, Leo says, will not only be a safeguard against modern error, but will also benefit the church at large, civil and domestic society (paras. 23, 28), as well as the arts and the physical sciences (para. 29). Just as there can be no real contradiction between the truths of faith and those attained by reason, Leo says there is no conflict between "the conclusions of modern physics and the philosophical principles of the schools" (para. 30). Although the pope makes clear the need for a return to "the golden wisdom of St. Thomas," he does not specify *what* interpretation of that wisdom is to be preferred, beyond insisting that "the doctrine of Thomas be drawn from his own fountains, or at least from those rivulets which, derived from that very fount, have thus far flowed, according to the established agreement of learned men, pure and clear" (para. 31). The story of Neothomism was to show that there was no such agreement.

What Leo had in mind with regard to "the rivulets derived from [Thomas's] very fount" was the view of Thomism put forth by his advisors, especially Kleutgen and Liberatore.[8] It is interesting that neither of these scholars wrote a commentary on the *Summa theologiae*, but rather expressed their Thomism in monographs, more philosophical in the case of Liberatore, more theological with Kleutgen. This is not to say that the era of lengthy commentaries on the

Summa was totally over, because the twentieth century was to see some examples of this genre among the Dominicans. Nevertheless, if the preferred genre of Second Thomism had been the commentary, the standard genre of Neothomism was the monographic analysis of some aspect of the thought of Thomas, primarily of a philosophical nature.

Liberatore's philosophical appropriation of Thomas emphasized the Dominican's realist epistemology based on abstraction from sense knowledge as opposed to the empiricism of Locke and the idealism of many German philosophers. He also denied that there was any direct intuition of the divine being, as some Catholic philosophers, such as the condemned Antonio Rosmini (d. 1855), had argued. Liberatore's vindication of Thomas's epistemology set forth in his *Della conoscenza intellettuale* (1857–58) and *Institutiones logicae et metaphysicae* (1860) set the groundwork for the Neothomistic attack on the Cartesian search for absolute certitude. Although the Italian's epistemology did reflect aspects of Thomas's views on knowing, he had little grasp of Thomistic metaphysics and its teaching on the importance of the act of existence. Kleutgen's two major works were *Die Theologie der Vorzeit* (*The Theology of Former Times*, i.e., before Descartes), five volumes published between 1853 and 1874, and *Die Philosophie der Vorzeit*, two volumes put out between 1860 and 1863. Kleutgen's view of the historical continuity of Catholic theology from its patristic roots down through the Middle Ages and culminating in Thomas was influential on *Aeterni Patris*. The German Jesuit's use of the history of theology gave Catholic apologists the sense that they had an effective argument against those who attacked the continuity of Catholic teaching over the centuries. Like Liberatore, Kleutgen contended that the great advantage of Thomist thought against modern error was the way the Angelic Doctor (as he was usually now referred to) was able to combine epistemology, anthropology, and metaphysics into a seamless whole. The core problem with Liberatore, Kleutgen, and other forms of what has been called "monumental Thomism" is that they were really replacing Thomas's *Summa* by rewriting it in a different historical context.[9]

The Growth of Neothomism

Had *Aeterni Patris* merely announced a program with no follow-up it would not have amounted to much. Pope Leo, however, caught the spirit of the time. His own efforts toward reviving Thomism were significant, but had these not been met by the fervor of Catholic intellectuals throughout the world, little might have been achieved. Neothomism rapidly became a popular movement, though a full explanation for its triumph remains unclear. Part of its success was due to the dissemination of Thomism throughout the Catholic seminary system.[10] Although the *Summa theologiae* itself appears not to have been much used as a class text outside Dominican universities and houses of study, the philosophical and theological manuals employed in seminaries circa 1880–1960 were generally based on Thomas, or at least purported to be *secundum mentem S. Thomae*, whatever that was taken to mean. A student of the North American College in Rome reflected the institutional triumph of Thomas in 1881 when he wrote to his bishop, Cardinal Gibbons of Baltimore, "every tongue has learned to lisp the new slang phrase in Rome: 'Ut ait Sanctus Doctor' ['as the Holy Doctor, i.e., St. Thomas, says']."[11] Although Thomism had become institutionally fashionable, there is no question that many also found it intellectually compelling. Of course, Thomas (unlike the writers of seminary manuals) was a major thinker, both philosophically and theologically, a point realized even by those who did not share his views. The American philosopher Josiah Royce (1855–1916) hailed the revival of Thomas in 1903 by remarking, "Pope Leo, after all, let loose a thinker among his people—a thinker, to be sure, of unquestioned orthodoxy, but after all a genuine thinker whom the textbooks had long tried, as it were, to keep lifeless, and who when once revived, proves to be full of suggestions of new problems and an effort toward new solutions."[12]

Along with *Aeterni Patris*, Leo XIII moved rapidly to implement the revival of Thomism. A papal letter of October 15, 1879, set up the Pontifical

Academy of Saint Thomas, one of whose tasks was to look into preparing a new edition of the works of the Angelic Doctor. On January 18, 1880, another papal document, *Placere nobis*, established what came to be called the Leonine Commission to undertake this task. Two other editions of the works of Thomas were produced in the nineteenth century, the twenty-five volume Parma edition of 1852–73, under the direction of Giovanni Maria Allodi, canon of the cathedral of Parma, and the thirty-four volume edition of Paris, the work of Louis Vivès and his collaborators (1871–82).[13] Neither of these editions, however, pretended to be a critical text; both were dependent on the original Piana edition of 1570 with a few corrections and emendations. The Leonine Edition had greater ambitions and an official role. Leo's Commission consisted of three cardinals, the Dominican Tommaso Zigliara, Antonio de Lucca, and Giovanni Simeoni. Their task was to produce a new version of the whole of Thomas's *Opera*, but the question soon emerged, what kind of an edition was this to be?

On this issue there was a difference of viewpoint between Pope Leo and the members of the commission.[14] Leo appears to have been emulating his predecessor Pius V in his desire to produce a sumptuous papal version of the *Opera Omnia* to further his program for the revival of Thomism. The members of the commission and their collaborators, however, were influenced by modern conceptions of critical editing that aimed at producing a text as faithful to the author's original as possible. From the beginning of the nineteenth century, German scholars connected with MGH (*Monumenta Germaniae Historica*) had worked out the philological and diplomatic skills for producing critical editions of medieval texts. The cardinals on the commission were not trained in these methods, but they enlisted the help of priests versed in editing, including the Dominican, Constantius Suermondt. The original plan was to begin with Thomas's philosophical works. Three volumes of these were published between 1882 and 1886, though these were scarcely of a critical character. Leo XIII, however, was not pleased. He wanted the *Summa theologiae*—the summit of Thomas's thought and the answer to modern errors—and he wanted it quickly. As Louis-Jacques Bataillon summarized, "The first concern of the editors was quality, but the pope's was celerity."[15] Leo ordered the editors to make use of the Piana text as the basis of the edition and utilize only manuscripts of the *Summa* found in the Vatican Library for corrections and variants. The harried editors got to work and managed to produce a defective edition of the *Prima Pars* in two large folio volumes published in 1888–89, as well as two volumes of the *Prima Secundae* in 1891–92. By that time Suermondt and his collaborators had begun to work out effective criteria for doing a more or less critical text of Thomas's works (not easy when there were more than four thousand manuscripts!). They also silently disregarded Leo's orders. Thus, the edition of the *Secunda Secundae* published 1895–99 marks a definite advance. The *Tertia Pars* and the *Supplementum* appeared in two volumes between 1903 and 1906. The Leonine edition of the *Summa theologiae*, therefore, is a kind of mélange—defective in its first half, somewhat better in the second. The *Summa* still lacks a rigorously critical text. The Leonine Commission, of course, has gone on to become one of the most distinguished of all medieval editing projects, producing meticulous editions of the other works of Thomas over more than a century. Its work looks to stretch on for decades to come, but it is not assured that the editors will come back to redo the *Summa*.

Concentrating the story of Neothomism on Rome does not give a full sense of the rapidity of the spread of Neoscholasticism/Neothomism throughout the Catholic world. A brief glance at some of the other centers of the Thomist revival, as well as at the new journals on Thomas and scholasticism can provide some sense of this. At the University at Louvain, one of the foremost centers of Catholic thought since the fifteenth century, a chair of Thomist philosophy was established in 1882 by the secular priest Desiré Joseph Mercier (1851–1926), later to become a cardinal. Mercier was interested in the relation between Thomism and modern philosophy and science, questions that were pursued at the Institute for Philosophy he established at Louvain in 1894. Thus, the Louvain form of Neothomism had a different tone from what was found in Rome. In France the Dominicans at both Paris and Toulouse returned to the study of Thomas in the 1880s, while in 1889 a Catholic faculty of theology was established at Fribourg in Switzerland and given to the Dominicans, who introduced a Thomist curriculum. Another measure of the success of Neothomism can be seen in the journals devoted to the study of Thomas and Neoscholasticism in general. These proliferated in the period between the first appearance of *Divus Thomas* in 1880 and the beginning of the American journal the *Thomist* in 1939. Another important step was the conversion of the Dominican House of Studies in Rome into a full-fledged papal university, the Angelicum (today the University of Saint Thomas) in 1909. In roughly a quarter century Neothomism had become *the* teaching of modern Catholicism.

Not everyone was happy with the triumph of Neoscholasticism and its ahistorical and antimodern mode of thought. The period 1890–1910 saw the growth of resistance to the regnant Neoscholasticism that sought to open Catholic philosophy, theology, and Biblical studies to contemporary thought, or at least to enter into dialogue with critical history, modern Biblical studies, and new philosophical currents. During these decades Catholic thinkers in France, England, Italy, and Germany sought a different approach to modernity. These scholars and thinkers were a varied lot engaged in many disciplines—for example, Alfred Loisy, Maurice

Blondel, and Lucien Laberthonnière in France; George Tyrrell and Friedrich von Hügel in England; Romolo Murri and Ernesto Buonaiuti in Italy; Franz Kraus and Josef Sauer in Germany. As different as they were in temperament and viewpoint, they came to be grouped together as "Modernists" by the reaction they provoked in Rome under the pontificate of Leo's successor, Pius X (1903–14).

The Modernists were too different in their interests to be described as constituting a movement with a single point of view.[16] "Modernism" was the creation of its opponents (Pius X and his ghostwriters). The Modernists were accused of many errors, such as (1) abandoning an objective and realist view of God for an agnostic, immanentist, and subjective philosophy; (2) an adherence to a historical outlook that saw the Bible as a merely human document and the evolution of Christian doctrine as only a reflection on religious experience; and (3) a consequent denial of the truth of many basic Christian beliefs, such as the divinity of Christ, in favor of a "symbolical" interpretation. The extent to which different Modernists did or did not hold these views remains under review. In 1907 Pope Pius issued a stinging condemnation of Modernism, first in a July 3 decree of the Holy Office titled *Lamentabili*, and then in the encyclical *Pascendi dominici gregis* of September 8, mostly written by the Oblate priest Joseph Lemius. *Pascendi* described Modernism as "the synthesis of all heresies . . . whose system means the destruction not of the Catholic religion alone, but of all religion." In 1910 Pius issued a decree that all the clergy would henceforth be obliged to take an oath against Modernism, the *Iusiurandum antimodernisticum*, which remained in force until Vatican II. Soon after, repressive measures were instituted throughout the Catholic world to identify, proscribe, and excommunicate not only the Modernist authors who may have held some of the positions attacked by the pope, but also all who might be conceived to have sympathized with them. An ecclesiastical reign of terror ensued, which, although it only lasted about fifteen years, rivaled later twentieth-century political witch hunts in its level of dishonesty and duplicity, though fortunately the Vatican no longer possessed any machinery of physical coercion, imprisonment, or worse. Among those secretly denounced, but not condemned, were Cardinal Mercier, the whole Dominican faculty at Fribourg, and the young priest Giuseppe Angelo Roncalli, the future Pope John XXIII.

The Encyclical *Pascendi* condemns the Modernists for wishing to relegate scholastic philosophy to the history of philosophy and teach modern philosophy in its stead in seminaries.[17] It also endorses Thomas Aquinas as the touchstone of truth, especially in metaphysics. There is no question that the major figures traditionally seen as Modernists identified the Neoscholasticism of *Aeterni Patris* as a key source of their complaints. Shortly after the publication of *Pascendi*, the Irish Jesuit George Tyrrel (1861–1909), soon to be excommunicated, wrote an open letter to the *Times* on September 30, 1907, in which he stated, "When the Encyclical tries to show the modernist that he is no Catholic, it mostly succeeds only in showing him he is no Scholastic, which he knew." Tyrrell's book *Medievalism* (1908), a response to Cardinal Mercier's attack on Modernism, amply demonstrates the opposition between the abstract, deductive, ahistorical mode of Neoscholastic thinking, on the one hand, and the historically minded, non-Aristotelian modes of philosophizing explored by many Modernists. But if Neoscholasticism was abhorrent to the Modernists, what did they think about Thomas himself?

The Modernists' views of Thomas were complicated, in part because the Modernists themselves were so different. Alfred Loisy (1857–1940), whose critical studies of the Bible and early church history made him perhaps the most prominent representative of Modernism, had read Thomas's *Summa* as a seminarian in the late 1870s and hated it. The same was true of the Modernist philosopher and theologian Lucien Laberthonièrre (1860–1932). The layman Friedrich von Hügel (1852–1925) also had little sympathy for Thomas. Tyrrell, on the other hand, read Thomas on his own as a seminarian in the 1880s and expressed his debt to the clarity and rigor of his thought, although under Von Hügel's influence he seems to have qualified this admiration late in his short life. The Dominican scripture scholar, Marie-Joseph Lagrange (1855–1938), long under a cloud as a Modernist but never condemned, was deeply formed by his Thomist education. The lay philosopher Maurice Blondel (1861–1949), also not formally condemned, appreciated the role that Thomism had served in its day, but worked toward finding a new more dynamic philosophy that would address the concerns of the present world. In general we can say that the Modernists disagreed with the program set out in *Aeterni Patris* regarding the revival of Scholasticism and its stress that a return to the "pure springs" of St. Thomas was the answer to all the problems of the day. Writing in the wake of *Pascendi*, Ernesto Buonaiuti (1881–1946) summarized this view in his *The Program of Modernism*: "Whence it is clear that it is impossible to impose religious experience on the modern mind in the same forms as were adapted to the utterly different mediaeval mind. The Church cannot, and ought not to, pretend that the *Summa* of Aquinas answers the exigencies of religious thought in the twentieth century."[18]

Pius X and his program of repression crushed Modernism—the movement that never was. Some Modernists voluntarily left the church or were driven out; others remained in the fold but kept a low profile. What did the crisis mean for the evolution of Thomism in the twentieth century? One effect seems to have been to expose how difficult it was for even the centralized modern papacy to control what kind of philosophy was to be taught in seminaries and especially in Catholic colleges. This is evident from the fact that for about a decade (1914–24), in part in reaction to the Modernist crisis, the Roman authorities issued document after document stressing that Thomism was the common teaching of the Church.

In a decree of June 29, 1914, titled *Doctoris Angelici*, Pius X insisted, once again, that "scholasticism" meant the teaching of Thomas Aquinas and that "all teachers of philosophy and sacred theology should be warned that if they deviated so much as one iota from Aquinas, especially in metaphysics, they exposed themselves to grave risk." Pius even went on to make the extraordinary claim that any commendation he or former popes had made of the doctrine of other writers and saints was true only to the extent that these writers had agreed with "the principles of Aquinas." Pius mandated that the *Summa theologiae* be used as the fundamental textbook in pontifical faculties. On July 27, 1914, the Sacred Congregation of Studies issued a list of twenty-four Thomistic theses *in philosophy* that must be adhered to in Catholic teaching. This list, which today appears slightly bizarre, was basically designed to de-legitimize the Suarezian reading of Thomas still favored by some Jesuits.[19] The twenty-four theses provoked a strong reaction on the part of the members of the Society of Jesus who still favored Suarezian Thomism. On March 7, 1916, another document from the Congregation of Studies backed off and declared the twenty-four theses to be only "sure directional norms." On March 19, 1917, Pius X's successor, Pope Benedict XV (1914–22), sent a letter to the Jesuit Superior General basically allowing the Jesuits to teach what they wanted to as long as they paid lip service to Thomas as the established teacher. "Twenty-Four-Thesis Thomism," however, remained a force in some Catholic philosophical institutions for decades.

The successors of Leo XIII and Pius X did not cease legislating Thomism as the official teaching of the Church. On June 29, 1923, the six-hundredth anniversary of Thomas's canonization, Pius XI (1922–39) issued an encyclical *Studiorum ducem* that hailed Thomas as "the common and universal Doctor of the Church, for the Church has adopted his philosophy for her very own, as innumerable documents of every kind testify." An Apostolic Constitution of May 24, 1931, also promulgated under Pius XI, laid down a detailed program of studies for all seminaries following a Thomist model. Papal insistence that Catholic training in philosophy and theology adhere to Thomas continued up to 1960 and Vatican II, though often in a more muted fashion. One prominent example was Pius XII's encyclical *Humani generis* of August 12, 1950, which might be described as the last gasp of monumental Neothomism. The encyclical warned against "dogmatic relativism" and condemned errors of recent theology, especially the so-called French "new theology" (*la nouvelle théologie*—like "Modernism" a pejorative term created by the Thomist opponents of new modes of theology). According to Pius XII, dangerous "innovators" had been led "from contempt of scholastic theology into forgetting or even despising the authority of the Church itself." The reason for these errors was the neglect of the scholastic philosophy of the Angelic Doctor, whose "philosophical system is an unrivalled method" and whose "teaching seems to chime in, by a kind of pre-established harmony, with divine revelation."[20] Despite Pius XII's insistence, however, the cutting edge of Catholic philosophy and theology had begun to move away from Neothomism in the 1930s and 1940s due to the growing realization that there was more to the Catholic tradition than scholasticism and that Thomas himself was far from a rigid thinker, or one whose meaning was always easily discernible.

The Neothomism enshrined in these papal documents of the first half of the twentieth century, aptly described as "monumental Thomism," "triumphalist Thomism," or "authoritarian Thomism," is just a memory today. Even as devoted a contemporary Thomist as the Dominican Jean-Pierre Torrell recently attacked it with vehemence, "What a strange reversal of fortunes! Resisted at its birth, and even condemned, Thomism, once made official, became a weapon in the hands of the authorities. . . . Imposed in an authoritarian way, Thomas's doctrine had nothing left of the creative force of the original."[21]

Contested Varieties of Thomism in the Twentieth Century

Pope Leo seemed to think that true Thomism could be found just by reading the text of Thomas with the help of the classic interpreters, which is why he insisted that Cajetan's commentary be reprinted along with the text of the *Summa* in the Leonine Edition. If history is barred from the front door, however, it has a way of sneaking in the back, as the story of the modern revival of Thomas and the *Summa* demonstrates. The contested varieties of Thomism that emerged in the first three quarters of the twentieth century show how difficult it was (and is) to find a single interpretation of a thinker as profound as Thomas. In many ways Neothomism nurtured the seeds of its own destruction almost from the start, especially because of its aversion to history. Due to the sheer amount of writing on Thomas in the twentieth century and also because we stand so close to this period, it is difficult to summarize this latest chapter in the story of the reception of Thomas and the *Summa theologiae.*[22]

It is not surprising that Dominicans and Jesuits were among the most influential interpreters of Thomas in the twentieth century; what was new was the emergence of lay Catholics, such as Jacques Maritain and Etienne Gilson—both of whom significantly eschewed being called "Neothomists." Attempting to categorize major philosophical and theological thinkers under specific headings is unfair to the subtleties of their thought, but useful for pedagogical purposes. I will use four general categories to provide a sense of twentieth-century Thomisms down to circa 1975: Strict-Observance Thomism, Revived Thomism, Metaphysical Thomism, and Transcendental Thomism. These categories are not to be thought of as discrete: a number of the figures mentioned could fit under several headings.

Strict-Observance Thomism came closest to what Leo XIII had in mind when he issued *Aeterni Patris*, that is, interpreting Thomas through the lens of the classic commentators, like Cajetan and John of St. Thomas, to establish a standard for Catholic teaching and the answer to the errors of modern thought. It flourished primarily in the first half of the twentieth century, and many of its foremost spokesmen were Dominicans, such as Ambrose Gardeil (1859–1931) and Reginald Garrigou-Lagrange (1877–1964). Gardeil, who was instrumental in the founding of the *Revue Thomiste* (begun in 1893) and in setting up the Dominican House of Studies at Le Saulchoir near Paris, was one of the earliest Thomists to attack the vitalistic philosophy of Henri Bergson (1859–1941) from the perspective of Thomism. His student Garrigou-Lagrange, whom the novelist François Mauriac once called "the Sacred Monster of Thomism," was among the most influential interpreters of Aquinas in the twentieth century.[23] Garrigou-Lagrange taught at the Angelicum in Rome from

1909 until 1959 and was deeply involved in Roman ecclesiastical and theological politics. He wrote extensively, including a series of monographic commentaries on sections of the *Summa theologiae* (e.g., *God, His Existence and Nature*). Garrigou-Lagrange was sure that Thomas had all the answers necessary to refute modern errors, and he was equally sure that he knew exactly what Thomas meant.[24] He was intensely polemical against what he saw as deviations from Thomas; it was he who coined the name "the new theology" (*la nouvelle théologie*) in 1946 to characterize what he felt were the errors of some French theologians, whom he accused of being halfway to the dread Modernism. Like his mentor Gardeil, Garrigou-Lagrange took a particular interest in spirituality and mysticism, lecturing on spirituality from 1917 until 1959. Although his approach to spirituality and mysticism is based on Thomas and John of St. Thomas, he also made use of mystics like John of the Cross.

Although the French *ressourcement* (literally, "resourcing") is usually associated with the theologians, mostly French Jesuits, who sought to go back behind scholasticism to recover the riches of the patristic tradition as a resource for modern theology, this form of reviving the past also fits those writers who worked toward a more adequate historical understanding of Thomas in the context of his own time and intentions. The need for a revived historical analysis of Thomas seems obvious today; it was

not for Leo XIII and classical Thomists. To introduce historical mindedness into the study of Thomas
was seen by some as bringing a Trojan horse into the
impregnable Neothomist fortress—which was true,
although not the whole truth.

Historical investigation of medieval philosophy began in the nineteenth century. Scholars soon
turned their attention to Thomas Aquinas. Among
the major pioneers in studying Thomas's life, as well
as the evolution and dating of his writings, was the
Dominican Pierre Mandonnet (1858–1936). His
work was continued in the later twentieth century by
other notable Dominican scholars. The major contribution of what I am calling "Revived Thomism"
came through both general and particular studies of
the historical meaning of Thomas. A central figure
in this endeavor was another French Dominican,
Marie-Dominique Chenu (1895–1990). Chenu studied with Garrigou-Lagrange in Rome, but turned
down an offer to be his successor at the Angelicum
to return to Le Saulchoir where Mandonnet and his
students were pursuing historical work on Thomas.
As a historical theologian, Chenu was interested not
just in establishing the details of Thomas's career, but
in investigating the significance of Thomas's theology
as a resource for contemporary thinking. Thomas
for him was not the author of a timeless speculative
system, but an example of how the Christian faith
achieves theological expression in diverse ages and
historical contexts. Without denying Thomas's use

of philosophy, Chenu correctly saw him as a theologian seeking the intelligibility of faith. "The very pith of his work," said Chenu, "was scriptural and his theology had its root in the Gospel movement of his day, just as it did the [theological] renaissance movement of which it was one of the effects. . . . Herein is the characteristic proper to scholastic theology, the abiding richness of the Thomistic system, the lovely fruit of the only renaissance that succeeded in the Western Christian world."[25]

Chenu became the head of Le Saulchoir in 1932 and in 1937 published a brochure titled *Une école de théologie: Le Saulchoir*, arguing for a historical approach to Thomas and criticizing the "Baroque Scholasticism" of Garrigou-Lagrange and the Angelicum. A donnybrook ensued. The Dominican Master General set up a commission to investigate the little book (Garrigou-Lagrange was one of the members), and Chenu's work was placed on the papal Index of Forbidden Books in 1942.[26] Although under a cloud, Chenu pursued his historical studies of Thomas and the *Summa*, training younger Dominicans, such as the ecclesiologist Yves Congar (1904–95). Chenu's 1939 paper on the structure of the *Summa* initiated modern discussion of this important topic, and in 1950 he produced his masterwork, *Introduction à l'étude de Saint Thomas d'Aquin* (English translation, 1964), an in-depth historical study of Thomas. Chenu went on to issue a second major work in 1957, a study of the twelfth-century theological renaissance that produced the world that made Thomas Aquinas possible, *La théologie au douzième siècle* (partial English translation, 1968). The French Dominican served as a theological advisor (*peritus*) at Vatican II and lived a long life in which he saw his historical-theological approach to Thomas vindicated by ongoing research.

Chenu was not alone in turning from ahistorical to historical investigation of Thomas and the scholastic world. The 1930s were the seedtime for the turn to history. Henri De Lubac (1896–1991), one of the leaders of the suspect "new theology" attacked by Garrigou-Lagrange, wrote about a wide range of theological issues, historical and contemporary. De Lubac was suspicious of the authoritarian Thomism of the time, but he too made a groundbreaking contribution to a more historical understanding of Thomas. From his student days, De Lubac had been interested in the question of how far the teaching about the supernatural character of human destiny put forth by the major Thomist commentators of the sixteenth century conformed to that found in Aquinas himself. He wrote various notes and papers on the topic over the years and in 1942 put these together into a manuscript called *Surnaturel. Études historiques*, though the book did not appear until 1946.[27] De Lubac showed that the notion of "pure nature" developed in Baroque scholasticism and dear to the Strict-Observance Thomists had no foundation in the thought of the Fathers, such as Augustine, and that it was a misreading of Thomas.

De Lubac's work was an example of a basic shift in the Catholic theology of the period circa 1935–60, one that turned away from the regnant Neothomist model in three major ways: (1) by rigorous historical investigation of what Thomas actually said within the context of the problems of his time; (2) by relativizing Thomas's position in the history of theology, seeing him as a significant figure but not as the ultimate authority on all issues; and (3) by engaging in a serious dialogue with modern forms of philosophy and non-Catholic theology.

Historical investigation of Thomas grew apace in the second half of the twentieth century through contributions by historians, philosophers, and theologians. The American Dominican James Weisheipl (1923–84), one of the foremost scholars of medieval philosophy and science, wrote much on Thomas, including a survey, *Friar Thomas D'Aquino. His Life, Thought, and Work* (1974), which remains one of the best general accounts. More recently, the French Dominican Jean-Pierre Torrell has contributed a host of studies, from specialized papers to impressive surveys. Another American, John Wippel of Catholic University, has become an important interpreter of Thomas's metaphysics.[28] The historical approach to Aquinas pioneered by Chenu and others, while certainly not the only approach, won the day, if not with ease, certainly with decisiveness.

It is not possible to separate historical studies of Thomas's thought from presentations of his philosophy designed to provide a challenge or alternative to contemporary philosophy: what I am calling "Metaphysical Thomism." Two of the most famous twentieth-century Thomist philosophers, Jacques Maritain and Etienne Gilson, illustrate the interaction of history and philosophy. Maritain (1882–1973) was primarily a philosopher, while Gilson (1884–1978) was a historian of medieval philosophy, but one who argued *philosophically* that Thomas's position was the best form of metaphysics. Although these two thinkers remained within the Neothomist paradigm that treated the Dominican primarily as a philosopher, Gilson recognized that Thomas's philosophy is found *within* his theology and that what he called Thomas's "Christian philosophy" was shaped by theological issues. Although the two Frenchmen were contemporaries, friends, and often linked in the popular mind, their views of Thomas were actually rather different.

Jacques Maritain, born a Protestant, converted to Catholicism under the influence of his teacher Henri Bergson. His first work on the philosophy of Bergson (1912) was a rejection of his mentor's vitalistic and evolutionary view of reality in favor of the realism of Thomas. Maritain's outpouring of works on every aspect of philosophy and what we would call today cultural studies was imbued with the traditional Thomism of Leo XIII, that is, Thomas as viewed through the classical commentators, especially Cajetan and John of St. Thomas. Nevertheless,

Maritain advanced the Thomist cause in important ways. First of all, more than any other modern Thomist, Maritain sought to realize Leo's agenda of employing Thomism to integrate the whole range of philosophy and science under the guiding influence of Thomist wisdom.[29] Adopting Cajetan's view of three degrees of Aristotelian abstraction (abstraction from individual matter in the realm of physics, abstraction from sensible matter in mathematics, and abstraction from all matter in metaphysics), Maritain argued for the autonomy of the various modes of knowledge, scientific and philosophic, within the wider natural integration of metaphysics and the supernatural integration provided by revelation. His integral philosophical perspective embraced an impressive range of topics on which he wrote with originality and passionate conviction: not only metaphysics and epistemology, but also art and poetry, prayer and mysticism, politics, and ethics and social issues. Maritain was resolutely opposed to Descartes and modern philosophy, insisting that the mind's immediate grasp of reality is the beginning of philosophy. His interpretation of Thomistic metaphysics as the study of being as achieved through what he called "eidetic visualization," that is, a kind of intuition of reality through the abstract form (*eidos* in Greek), was laid out in his *Preface to Metaphysics* (1934), and especially in *Existence and the Existent. An Essay on Christian Existentialism* (1948). Maritain's most ambitious book, *Distinguish to Unite, or The Degrees of Knowledge* (1933), sought to integrate a Thomist understanding of the kinds of rational knowing found in science and philosophy with the supra-rational knowing available through grace and mystical experience, using John of the Cross. Nevertheless, this work shows that Maritain's view of Thomas was primarily absorbed through John of St. Thomas's teaching, not that of Thomas himself.

Like Maritain, Etienne Gilson came to Thomism by a circuitous route.[30] He began his studies at the Sorbonne under the sociologist and philosopher Emile Durkheim in the midst of the excitement over the philosophy of Bergson. Gilson had not even read Aquinas when in 1905 Lucien Lévy-Bruhl suggested he write a dissertation on Descartes and the scholastics. In the course of writing this work (published in 1913) Gilson discovered Thomas. In 1913–14 he gave a series of lectures on Thomas that eventually appeared as the first edition of *Le Thomisme*, of which he later wrote, "The book deserves to survive in this first edition as a monument to the ignorance of its author."[31] But Gilson persisted in his study of Thomas and the whole medieval tradition. His impressive series of works on the thought of many medieval thinkers (e.g., Augustine, Bonaventure, Duns Scotus, and Bernard), eventually summarized in his massive *History of Christian Philosophy in the Middle Ages* (1955), as well as a host of papers and other studies, made him the foremost twentieth-century interpreter of the intellectual tradition of the Middle Ages. Gilson recognized the variety that characterized medieval thinkers, but also argued for a fundamental unity of the medieval intellectual tradition under the rubric of "Christian philosophy," which he saw, in good Thomist fashion, as the kind of philosophy developed by medieval theologians through the use of reason in investigating both the truths of faith and those that can be discovered by reason itself. Gilson first set out his view of the unity in diversity of medieval thought in his *The Spirit of Medieval Philosophy* (Gifford Lectures for 1931–32).

Gilson agreed with Leo XIII and the tradition of Strict-Observance Thomism that Thomas's Christian philosophy represented the acme of medieval Christian philosophy, especially because of what Gilson referred to as "the Metaphysics of the Exodus," that is, Thomas's breakthrough to a philosophy based on God as *ipsum esse subsistens*, the pure act of existence revealed by the divine voice in Exodus 3:14, saying "I am who am." The God of Exodus is the One whose Essence is identical with Existence itself and the Creator of all beings whose essence is not the same as existence, but who exist in particular ways as angels, humans, animals, and so on. Gilson appears to have made this breakthrough in his thinking on Thomas around 1940, since it appears in his book *God and Philosophy* (1941) and was incorporated into the fourth edition of *Le Thomisme* of 1942, as well as the definitive fifth edition, translated as *The Christian Philosophy of St. Thomas Aquinas* (1956).

Gilson's metaphysics of the Exodus was summarized in his major philosophical work, *Being and Some Philosophers* (1949), in which he contrasts Thomas's philosophy of Being as Existence with the opposed views of metaphysics based on the supremacy of the One (Platonists), of Substance (Aristotle and the Arabs), and of Essence (most modern philosophers and many so-called Thomists). Gilson's books initiated lengthy discussions about the nature of Christian philosophy.[32] Toward the end of his career in his memoir, *The Philosopher and Theology*, Gilson clarified his idea of Christian philosophy and its relation to theology, laying greater stress on the necessity for a theological perspective as the originating element: "The most original notions, and the deepest, in the doctrine of St. Thomas reveal themselves only to him who reads it as a theologian."[33]

Gilson's recovery of the core of Thomas's metaphysics was not an individual breakthrough, but was part of a general movement among students of Aquinas in the 1930s and 1940s. Other investigators of Thomas and the *Summa* also freed themselves from the essentialist interpretation of Thomas's view of being found in the classic commentators and early Neothomism to realize that not only was the act of existence the heart of the Dominican's view of reality, as Gilson affirmed, but also the notion of participation in existence (something he neglected) was a key to unlocking Thomas's understanding of God as creator. Among the first in the field was Joseph de

Finance, whose book *Être et agir dans la Philosophie de Saint Thomas* (*Existence and Action in the Philosophy of St. Thomas*) was written 1927–38, but not published until 1946 due to World War II. As he put it in the Preface to the second edition, "On the Thomist notion of *esse*, after many converging studies the agreement seems about to be realized today. More and more clearly the original contribution of St. Thomas is located in the relation of *esse* as existential actuation and of *esse* as a fullness limited by essence."[34] De Finance recognized that this limitation of *esse* was a form of participation, but it was left to several other thinkers to work out more detailed evaluations of how Thomas incorporated Platonic and Neoplatonic participation themes into his metaphysics. Cornelio Fabro published *La nozione metafisica della partecipazione secondo San Tommaso d'Aquino* (*The Metaphysical Notion of Participation according to Saint Thomas*) in 1939. A somewhat different view of Thomist participation was put forth by L.-B. Geiger in his *La participation dans la philosophie de S. Thomas d'Aquin* (*Participation in the Philosophy of Saint Thomas Aquinas*) published in 1942.[35]

The historical and metaphysical retrievals of Thomas's thought from the 1930s and 1940s are to be distinguished from another movement in the modern reception of Thomism, one more radical, which sought to put Thomas into conversation with modern philosophy, especially the Kantian philosophy of the turn to the subject, as well as the emphasis on intuition and action found in the thought of Bergson and Blondel. This attempt to create a conversation between Thomas and modern philosophy was anathema for Garrigou-Lagrange, as well as for Maritain and Gilson: If Thomism gave away its objective sense of external reality founded on sense knowing, how could it not succumb to the subjectivism and relativism that popes from the early nineteenth century on had feared would be the end of Catholic truth?[36] Early in the twentieth century some Jesuit philosophers and theologians began to wonder if it might be possible to investigate what Thomas had to say about how the human subject attains truth, that is, to start with Thomas's a priori, or fundamental, conditions for knowing, even when these were not always explicitly set out by Thomas himself, in order to create a dialogue with the subjective turn of modern philosophy. In their view, Thomas's epistemology, investigated from within the framework of the critical method, might provide a way out of the impasse between modern philosophy and Catholic thought. This approach came to be called "Transcendental Thomism," though the name was not created by its supposed proponents.[37]

The beginnings of this new form of Thomism can be traced to 1908. In that year the Jesuit Pierre Rousselot (1878–1915) published his dissertation *L'Intellectualisme de Saint Thomas* (*The Intellectualism of Saint Thomas*).[38] For Rousselot intellectualism is "the doctrine which places the supreme value and intensity of life in an act of the intellect," but this was not to be conceived of, as so often with the classical Thomists, as abstractive concept formation and deductive reasoning. Rather, true Thomist intellectualism is rooted in the primacy of contemplation, that act by which the mind's dynamism is directed to the beatific vision. Rousselot summarized this by saying, "Intelligence, for St. Thomas, is the faculty of the real, but it is the faculty of the real only because it is the faculty of the divine."[39] Rousselot says that God alone realizes the identity of pure idea and living spirit in a supreme act of intuition; human knowing, tied to material reality but directed to the intuitive grasp of God as its end, strives to simulate and supplement the perfection of intuitive knowing through the formation of concepts and the creation of science, system, and symbols in human speculation. In this original book Rousselot refrained from investigating what Thomas had to say about the act of judgment, but he soon sensed that he had been mistaken in this omission by reading the articles of a fellow Jesuit, the Belgian Joseph Maréchal (1878–1944), who taught at Louvain.

Maréchal was trained in biology and empirical psychology, as well as philosophy and theology. The important paper that influenced Rousselot's later work, published in 1908 and 1909 and titled "The Feeling of Presence in Mystics and Non-Mystics,"[40] was an attempt to show that a philosophical analysis of the nature of human knowing is needed to complete and correct the findings of empirical psychology concerning mystical states of intuition of God. Maréchal's argument rests upon his analysis of the a priori conditions for the possibility of a judgment of presence, which is also a judgment of reality. For the Belgian Jesuit, "The judgment of reality is a synthesis which is not justified solely by itself," but is rather rooted in the nature of the human mind as a *"faculty in quest of its intuition*—that is to say, of assimilation with Being, Being pure and simple, sovereignly *one*, without restriction, without distinction of essence and existence, of possible and real."[41] At this point, Maréchal, not surprisingly, footnotes a number of texts from Aquinas, and, indeed, he closes off the article with the statement, "We judge that the hypothesis is *psychologically* acceptable. And this was of old the opinion of St. Thomas Aquinas. We have hardly done more than interpret his doctrine."[42]

Maréchal's lifting up of the act of judgment as central to Thomas's intellectualism was to bear fruit in his massive five-volume "Notebooks" (*Cahiers*) titled *Le point de depart de la métaphysique. Leçons sur le développement historique et théorique du problème de la connaissance*, published between 1922 and 1926. Volume 5, bearing the title *Le Thomisme devant la philosophie critique* (*Thomism in the Face of Critical Philosophy*), sought to mediate the conflict between Thomist realism and Kant's insistence that the human mind can never attain real things (*noumena*), but knows phenomena only as received in the transcendental categories of space and time. For Maréchal the noumenal, or real, character of the finite essences affirmed in the act of judgment is revealed in the dynamic structure of the very act of affirmation, which is directed toward Absolute Being as the goal of its nature. Gerald McCool sees a close affinity between the positions argued by Rousselot and Maréchal: "Both of them felt that, properly understood and consistently applied, Kant's transcendental method could vindicate a Thomistic metaphysics of man and being. Maritain and Gilson, on the other hand, remained firmly convinced that Thomist realism and post-Cartesian epistemology were radically incompatible. Any attempt on the part of a Thomist to 'go in Kant's door and come out his own' was completely misguided."[43] Maréchal's engagement with modern philosophy, however, was to bear fruit in other Jesuits who were influenced by the Belgian and sought to rethink aspects of Thomas's thought within a modern context.

In the late 1930s the Canadian Jesuit Bernard Lonergan (1904–84) began work at the Gregorian University on Thomas's understanding of operating grace (*gratia operans*). Lonergan published his dissertation as a series of articles in the American journal *Theological Studies* in 1941–42 and later in book form.[44] Through a meticulous analysis of Thomas's developing thought on grace and freedom culminating in the treatment in the *Summa*, Lonergan was able to show that Thomas's theory "stands as a higher synthesis to the opposition of later theories," that is, the warring sixteenth-century views on grace and freedom found in the schools of Dominican Bane- zianism and Jesuit Molinism. Lonergan's engage- ment with Thomas's doctrine of grace was part of a more ambitious rethinking of the Dominican's teaching on knowing that Lonergan said was inspired by reading Maréchal's *Cahiers*. The first fruits of this came in another study of Thomas, this time devoted to his understanding of *verbum*, the inner word of understanding which, Lonergan argued, is the cen- ter of Thomist epistemology and crucial for grasp- ing his Trinitarian theology (Ia, q. 27). Once again, Lonergan argued that Thomas achieved a higher viewpoint that was able to combine an Augustin- ian phenomenology of the subject with an Aristo- telian psychology of the soul.[45] Lonergan admitted that his argument put together scattered materials found in Thomas and so he described it as "Thomis- tic but hardly Thomist." One can see the background in Maréchal when Lonergan says that his analysis of the act of judgment shows that "this act consists in a grasp of the native infinity of the intellect; for on the one hand, Thomist thought does stress that native infinity, and, on the other hand, from such infin- ity one can grasp the capacity of the mind to know reality."[46] Lonergan's retrieval of Thomas on the act of understanding was the basis for the development of his own cognitional theory in his masterwork, *Insight. A Study of Human Understanding* (1957), a work that is not about Thomas in any direct way, but, Lonergan insisted, was a development of Thomas's epistemology within the contemporary philosophical context.

Lonergan's contemporary, the German Jesuit Karl Rahner (1904–84), took a different route to his version of what he once called "'transcendentally-tainted' philosophical Thomism."[47] Rahner's earliest writings were on mystical theology, but in the mid-1930s, while studying philosophy at the Jesuit house at Pullach, he recounts, "I read with extraordinary eagerness and great care the fifth volume by Joseph Maréchal, S. J., *Le point de depart de la métaphysique.*" Rahner claims that this encounter was at the origin of what others later called "transcendental philosophy and theology," so that, "To the extent that this Maréchalianism stems from Thomas and to the extent that Maréchal again and again tries to prove his thought through Thomas, I can say that Thomism formed my philosophy and, at a step removed, my theology."[48] Not everyone was convinced about the authenticity of this reading of Aquinas. When Rahner went off a few years later to study philosophy at Freiburg under Martin Heidegger and Martin Honecker, the thesis he prepared on Thomas's theory of knowledge, specifically on what the Dominican meant by "conversion to the phantasm" (Ia, q. 84.7) as integral to human knowing, was not accepted by Honecker due to its radical interpretation of Thomas. Completed in 1936 and published in 1939, this work, *Spirit in the World* (English version 1967), is rightly seen as central to Rahner's later immense output. Rahner did not intend to write a historical study of Thomas, but rather a reliving of Thomas's "philosophy as it unfolds," which, not unlike Lonergan, pushed Thomas beyond what he explicitly says, but in a direction that the author still claims is what Thomas *would* have said in the post-Kantian philosophical world.

Rahner and Lonergan had distinctive theological agendas that can be distorted by grouping them under the umbrella of Transcendental Thomism. Rahner learned from Thomas that theology necessarily implies philosophy, but his use of Thomas might be described as piecemeal, a picking and choosing of Thomas, especially in cases where his insights had been forgotten over the centuries. Rahner was also ready to criticize Thomas, for example, in relation to the setting and development of Aquinas's Trinitarian theology in the *Summa*. Lonergan, on the other hand, insisted that his subsequent philosophical and theological writings were developed out of insights he gained from reading Thomas, although he claimed that the Thomism of the future would need to be radically recast in the light of the shift from the static and ahistorical "classical worldview" inherited from Aristotle that shaped much of Thomas's thought to the historical mindedness of the present, a shift he described as the transition from logic to method. Both Rahner and Lonergan abandoned the imperialistic Neothomism of Leo XIII and even that of Maritain and Gilson in favor of a pluralistic conversation among many philosophical and theological voices. These two major figures of twentieth-century Catholic theology cannot be understood without attention to how Thomas and his *Summa* helped shape their thought.

The third of the Catholic theologians who dominated the middle and late twentieth century was the Swiss Hans Urs von Balthasar (1905–88). Despite the fact that von Balthasar wrote an impressive study of Thomas's view of charismatic graces and contemplation,[49] his thought was much less formed by Thomas. Von Balthasar's great contribution was a massive trilogy of multivolume works: *The Glory of the Lord* treating theological aesthetics in seven volumes (1961–69), *Theo-Drama* on divine and human action in five volumes (1973–83), and *Theo-Logic* in three volumes (1985–87). *Theo-Drama* contains von Balthasar's sustained reflections on Christian doctrines, but given how different von Balthasar's ordering of Christian doctrine is from Thomas's *Summa theologiae*, it is somewhat surprising when the introductory note to the final volume says, "Following Aquinas, we have tried to erect theology on the articles of faith (and not vice versa)."[50] In his treatment of "Metaphysics in Antiquity" in volume 4 of *The Glory of the Lord*, von Balthasar supports Thomas's metaphysics of the act of being (*actus essendi*) as representing a decisive shift (*kairos*) from ancient thought that both "opens our eyes to the truth that God is self-subsistent being but . . . also closes our eyes and forbids us to cling to what we have seen."[51] Von Balthasar, however, was scarcely a Thomist.

The new theological voices that surfaced in the 1930s and 1940s had a key role in the Second Vatican Council that met between 1962 and 1965. The original documents for the sessions prepared in Rome according to the usual Neoscholastic theology were mostly rejected out of hand, so commissions of bishops and theological experts prepared new draft documents that would reflect the church's attempt to fulfill Pope John XXIII's desire for an "updating" (*aggiornamento*) of Roman Catholicism's relation to contemporary society.[52] Thomas Aquinas was not forgotten, cited 734 times in the Decrees and Documents of Vatican II, far more than any other authority (Augustine is next with 522 citations). Vatican II was a pastoral rather than a dogmatic council, one based not on confrontation with modernity, but on an attempt to reach out to people of good will. Above all, it was not set forth in the rigid scholastic language of deductive certainty based on irrefutable principles, but on a dialogical language of rhetorical engagement. It is not surprising that with the Council the Neoscholasticism, especially in its Neothomist variety, that had appeared so powerful even in the 1950s vanished almost overnight—it had been hollowed out from within for decades.

The decade following the Council down to 1974, the seven hundredth anniversary of the death of Thomas Aquinas (and also of Bonaventure), was a time of turmoil and contention, both in the Catholic Church and in Western society, as witnessed in the reaction to the papal ban on artificial birth control in 1968 and the radical student upheavals in Europe and the United States in 1968–69. Serious differences of opinion and cultural divides were created then that are still strong today. These have had their effect on Thomism and the reception of the *Summa*, but in ways that may still be too present to be fully understood as yet. A curriculum based on (or pretending to be based on) Thomas Aquinas rapidly disappeared from Catholic higher education, but this did not mean that the study of Thomas was at an end. The monolithic Thomism that Leo XIII and his followers hoped would stem the tides of atheism, rationalism, subjectivism, fideism, and other errors faded both in official Roman Catholic teaching and in the world of scholarship. On the official side, papal support was still offered for Thomas, but within a theological world that admitted a pluralism of approaches to the understanding of faith. The anniversary of the deaths of Thomas and Bonaventure was greeted by a host of celebrations, conferences, and jamborees held throughout the Catholic world. The number of pages produced in the publications from these events certainly surpassed that of the *Summa* itself and added much to what we know about Thomas, his world, and his thought.[53] Nevertheless, few of the authors of these studies were still holding up Thomas as the cure for all the ills of the modern world. Even Pope Paul VI, who sent a letter titled *Lumen Ecclesiae* to the Master of the Dominican Order for the event, did not do more than recommend "authentic fidelity to Thomas" for the saint's own order.

It would take a long chapter to try to do justice to the varieties of Thomism and the forms of reception of the *Summa theologiae* that have proliferated since the anniversary of Thomas's death in 1974. Though Neothomism seems dead, many other forms of Thomism are alive and well, as Neothomism's end sparked a new generation of historical, philosophical, and theological retrievals of the *Summa*, so varied as to defy generalization. Thus, Fergus Kerr recently referred to "the diversity and incommensurability of the available interpretations of Thomas's work" as a characteristic of our time.[1]

In the decades since 1974 the official voice of Roman Catholicism has continued to recommend Thomas Aquinas, but in a different way from what was found between 1879 and 1965. The new Code of Canon Law promulgated under Pope John Paul II in 1983 speaks of Thomas as a teacher especially endowed for leading students into the depths of the mysteries of salvation, though without any insistence on the supremacy of the Angelic Doctor. *The Cate-chism of the Catholic Church* issued in 1994 refers to Thomas sixty-one times, especially from the *Summa theologiae*, second only to Augustine, who is cited eighty-seven times. The most important recent papal document for the revised status of Thomas is the 1998 Encyclical *Fides et Ratio* of John Paul II, him-self a former professor of philosophy. Several times in the document John Paul refers back to *Aeterni Patris* as a model for his thinking, but there is also an evident contrast between Leo's encyclical and John Paul's. John Paul insists that while there is a necessary connection between theology and philosophical rea-soning, there can be no single philosophy taught by the Church. Speaking of Christian philosophy, he says, "[T]he term is valid, but it should not be mis-understood: it in no way suggests that there is an offi-cial philosophy of the Church, since faith as such is not a philosophy. The term seeks rather to indicate a Christian way of philosophizing."[2] Many forms of philosophy are useful, though none is totally ade-quate. Thomas's thought is mentioned with approval more often than others,[3] but only as an example of how to go about trying to relate the demands of phi-losophy and theology—"Thomas is an authentic model for all who seek the truth" (sec. 78)—not the thinker who provides the answer to all questions.

The demise of triumphal Thomism has been a boon for historical study of Thomas, as well as philo-sophical and theological engagement of Thomas's thought free from ideological concerns. In the words of Otto Hermann Pesch, Thomas has finally been released from house arrest. In the wake of Vatican II, therefore, Thomas has played a more restricted role in Catholic theology than he enjoyed in the first half of the twentieth century, but the new historical and contextual work on Thomas has been fruitful for uncovering the true contours of his thought and seeing its place in the broader tradition. In recent decades scholars have produced insightful studies of specific themes of Thomas's theology, especially in the *Summa*, as well as several good introductions to Thomas as theologian. One area that has emerged with special force has been the recognition that Thomas's *Summa theologiae*, despite its rigorous form of argumentation, is a work rooted in deep spiritual insight.[4]

Philosophical engagement with Thomas and the *Summa* has continued to be a lively area of research and writing, despite greater awareness that Thomas was actually a professor of theology and that attempts to create a Thomistic philosophy are always new endeavors based on aspects of Thomas's thought. What is obvious is that Thomas's way of engaging rational argumentation in the service of understanding faith provides a resource for philosophers and philosophical theologians to enter into dialogue with him on the perennial issue of the relation of faith and reason. This is a tribute to the ongoing power of Thomas's thought, especially as seen in his two masterworks, *Summa theologiae* and *Summa contra Gentiles*. Just as the writings of great philosophers like Immanuel Kant and Henri Bergson inspired studies of the relation of their philosophies and the thought of Thomas, in recent decades there have been attempts to put Thomas into conversation with major twentieth-century philosophers such as Martin Heidegger (1889–1976) and Ludwig Wittgenstein (1889–1951). Some Anglo-American analytic philosophers have found in Thomas a useful resource for thinking about how language relates to claims about God and reality. This "Analytical Thomism," as it has been called, persists in England and in North America.[5] There is still a danger, however, in treating Thomas more as a philosopher than as a theologian, or in mistaking his intentions.

This is not the place to try to review the many forms of Thomism that have appeared in recent decades. A longer book might look at the survival of "Palaeo-Thomism," roughly what I referred to as Strict-Observance Thomism. (A variant I recently heard of was termed "Taliban-Thomism.") Other new approaches to Thomas include Radical-Orthodox Thomism, Postliberal Thomism, Postmodern Thomism, and the like. Over the past generation a number of distinguished scholars of Thomas have gazed into their crystal balls to make predictions about what the future of Thomism might hold.[6] I will forego any attempt at this. It is difficult enough to try to provide an evaluation of the impact of figures over the past century on the history of the reception of the *Summa*, let alone to presage the direction that new study of Thomas's great work might take. One thing that does seem sure, however, is that Thomas and his *Summa theologiae* will remain an important part of philosophical and theological discussion in the Western tradition. The cycle of wisdom rolls on.

Abbreviations for Frequently
Cited Works of Thomas Aquinas

STh
 Summa theologiae (Summa of Theology)
SCG
 Summa contra Gentiles (Summa against the Pagans)
Comp. theol.
 Compendium theologiae (Compendium of Theology)
In Sent.
 Scriptum super libros sententiarum (Writing on the Sentences of Peter Lombard)
De ver.
 Quaestiones disputatae de veritate (Disputed Questions on Truth)
De pot.
 Quaestiones disputatae de potentia Dei (Disputed Questions on the Power of God)
De malo
 Quaestiones disputatae de malo (Disputed Questions on Evil)
Quod.
 Quaestiones de quodlibet (Questions on Various Topics)
De Trinitate
 Expositio super librum Boethii "De Trinitate" (Commentary on Boethius's "On the Trinity")

INTRODUCTION

1. IaIIae, q. 66.5; see also q. 57.2, and q. 68.7. Following Aristotle (*Nicomachean Ethics* 6.7), Thomas identifies three speculative habits: understanding (*intellectus*), the habit that deals with principles; science (*scientia*), the habit that deals with conclusions; and wisdom (*sapientia*), the habit that deals with both principles and conclusions and therefore orders and judges the others.

2. See Ia, q. 43.5, ad 2; and IIaIIae, q. 45.2.

3. *SCG* II. 46. Thomas also notes the role of the Incarnation as essential to the circular movement of going forth and returning; see *In III Sent.*, prol., and *Comp. theol.* 201.

4. On wisdom in Aquinas, Jacques Maritain, *Science and Wisdom* (New York: Scribner, 1940), pt. 1; Etienne Gilson, *Wisdom and Love in Saint Thomas Aquinas* (Milwaukee: Marquette University Press, 1951); and Kieran Conley, *A Theology of Wisdom. A Study in St. Thomas* (Dubuque, IA: Priory Press, 1963).

CHAPTER 1 The World That Made Thomas Aquinas

1. Bernard J. F. Lonergan, "The Future of Thomism," in *A Second Collection*, William Ryan and Bernard Tyrrell, eds. (Philadelphia: Westminster Press, 1974), 44.

2. On the development, Stephen C. Ferruolo, *The Origins of the University: The Schools at Paris and Their Critics, 1100–1215* (Stanford: Stanford University Press, 1985).

3. For a sketch of the three basic varieties of medieval theology—monastic, scholastic, and vernacular—Bernard McGinn, "*Regina quondam . . . ,*" *Speculum* 83 (2008): 817–39.

4. The foundational study remains Martin Grabmann, *Die Geschichte der scholastischen Methode*, 2 vols. (Freiburg im Breisgau: Herder, 1909–11).

5. Beryl Smalley's *The Study of the Bible in the Middle Ages* (Oxford: Blackwell, 1940) was the first to draw attention to this.

6. Fernand Van Steenberghen, *Aristotle in the West: Origins of Latin Aristotelianism* (Louvain: Nauwelaerts, 1955).

7. On Dominic and the early Dominicans, Simon Tugwell, *Early Dominicans. Selected Writings* (New York: Paulist Press, 1982).

8. Humbert of Romans, *Treatise on the Formation of Preachers* I.82, in Tugwell, *Early Dominicans*, 205.

CHAPTER 2 The Making of the *Summa theologiae*

1. James A. Weisheipl, *Friar Thomas d'Aquino. His Life, Thought, and Work* (Garden City, NY: Doubleday, 1974); and Jean-Pierre Torrell, *Saint Thomas Aquinas. Vol. 1, The Person and His Work* (Washington, DC: Catholic University Press, 1996). See also Simon Tugwell, "Thomas Aquinas: Introduction," in *Albert and Thomas. Selected Writings* (New York: Paulist Press, 1988), 201–351.

2. Not long after the accession to the papacy of John XXII (1316) the Naples Province of the Dominicans began the process that culminated in Thomas's canonization on July 18, 1323. Three lives of Thomas were written by Dominicans. The oldest was that of William of Tocco, edited by Claire le Brun-Gouanvic, *Ystoria sancti Thome de Aquino*

de Guillaume de Tocco (1323) (Toronto: PIMS, 1996). We also have the records of the two canonization inquiries (Naples 1319 and Fossanova 1321). Some of these materials are available in *The Life of St. Thomas Aquinas. Biographical Documents*, by Kenelm Foster (London: Longmans, Green, 1959).

3. This story appears in almost all the sources and, according to the hagiographers, was accompanied by a dream vision guaranteeing Thomas's lifelong chastity.

4. Tocco, *Ystoria*, Chap. 13 (ed., 117–18).

5. Ibid., chap. 15 (ed., 122).

6. Thomas's inception lecture, "Rigans montes de superioribus suis," is translated in Tugwell, *Albert and Thomas*, 355–60.

7. Thomas's most important defense of the mendicants is his 1256 treatise *Against Those Attacking the Worship of God and Religion*.

8. *On the Perfection of the Spiritual Life*, chap. 26.

9. *De ver.* consists of qq. 1–20 dealing with truth and knowledge, and qq. 21–29 treating the good and appetite. For an English translation: *St. Thomas, On Truth*, 3 vols. (Chicago: Regnery, 1952–54).

10. Thomas's hagiographers testify to the effectiveness of his preaching; see Tocco, *Ystoria*, chap. 48 (ed., 182–84).

11. For a recent interpretation of the importance of unicity of form in Thomas's thought, Denys Turner, *Thomas Aquinas* (New Haven: Yale University Press, 2013), 62–69.

12. Like most medieval people, Thomas had a strong faith in relics and is said to have worn around his neck a relic of St. Agnes, which he once used to cure Brother Reginald of a dangerous fever. In honor of this miracle he ordered that the brothers be given a good meal on the anniversary of the event.

13. See the account in the First Canonization Inquiry, no. 78, as translated by Foster, *Life of St. Thomas Aquinas*, 108–9.

14. First Canonization Inquiry, no. 77 (Foster, *Life of St. Thomas Aquinas*, 107).

15. First Canonization Inquiry, no. 79 (Foster, *Life of St. Thomas Aquinas*, 109).

16. Weisheipl, *Friar Thomas D'Aquino*, 321–23; Torrell, *Saint Thomas Aquinas*, 1:289–95.

17. This story is part of the testimony of Bartholomew of Capua in the First Canonization Inquiry, no. 77 (Foster, *Life of St. Thomas Aquinas*, 108).

18. The lives of Thomas and the two canonization investigations are filled with miracle stories, though perhaps not as many as those recorded of many other medieval saints. Pope John XXII, when questioned if there were enough miracles for Thomas's canonization, is alleged to have responded, "He performed as many miracles as articles he wrote" (*tot fecerat miracula quot scripserat articulos*).

19. The story about Thomas dictating different works at the same time is found in Tocco, *Ystoria*, chap. 18 (ed., 134–35). According to the testimony of one of his scribes, Evan Garnit, Thomas was able to continue dictating even while asleep!

20. The most recent survey of Thomas's writings is by Gilles Emery in Torrell, *Saint Thomas Aquinas*, 1:330–61.

21. First Canonization Inquiry, no. 83 (Foster, *Life of St. Thomas Aquinas*, 114).

22. For a good introduction, Jean-Pierre Torrell, *Aquinas's Summa. Background, Structure, & Reception* (Washington, DC: Catholic University Press, 2005).

23. In the early twelfth century *summa* signified a collection of materials, but by the thirteenth century it had come to mean an ordered presentation. Many thirteenth-century scholastics wrote *summae*; e.g., William of Auxerre, Alexander of Hales, Roland of Cremona, John of Trevisa, Albert the Great, and, after Thomas, Ulrich of Strassburg and Henry of Ghent.

24. This calculation is given in Torrell, *Aquinas's* Summa, 14.

25. Given its length, it is not surprising that the almost six hundred manuscripts of the *STh* indicate that the three parts often circulated independently, as shown by Leonard E. Boyle, *The Setting of the "Summa Theologiae" of Saint Thomas* (Toronto: PIMS, 1982). The *Secunda Pars* was the most popular.

26. On the Dominican program of education, M. Michèle Mulchahey, *"First the Bow Is Bent in Study." Dominican Education before 1350* (Toronto: PIMS, 1998), especially 278–306 on Thomas's Santa Sabina years.

27. The case for Santa Sabina being an unusual *studium personale* was first made by Boyle, *Setting of the "Summa Theologiae."*

28. Parts of this *alia lectura* exist in an Oxford manuscript edited by Leonard E. Boyle and John F. Boyle, *Lectura romana in primum Sententiarum Petri Lombardi* (Toronto: PIMS, 2006).

29. Thomas cites the Pseudo-Dionysius 1,702 times in his works, 562 times in the *Summa*, according to Torrell, *Aquinas's Summa*, 78. See Fran O'Rourke, *Pseudo-Dionysius and the Metaphysics of Aquinas* (Notre Dame: University of Notre Dame Press, 2005).

30. Mulchahey, *"First the Bow Is Bent,"* 278–306, affirms he did; Torrell, *Saint Thomas Aquinas*, 1:145–47, thinks it likely. Thomas's teaching of the *Summa* is denied by James Weisheipl, "The Meaning of *Sacra Doctrina* in *Summa Theologiae* I, q. 1," *Thomist* 38 (1974): 49–80; and Mark D. Jordan, "The *Summa's* Reform of Moral Teaching—and Its Failures," in *Contemplating Aquinas. On the Varieties of Interpretation*, Fergus Kerr, ed. (Notre Dame: University of Notre Dame Press, 2003), 41–54, especially 44–46, 52–54.

31. On the two levels of Aristotelian *scientia*, John J. Jenkins, *Knowledge and Faith in Thomas Aquinas* (Cambridge:

Cambridge University Press, 1997), 46–49; on Thomas's intended audience as advanced students, see chap. 3, and 215–19.

32. See, for example, Boyle, *Setting of the "Summa Theologiae"*; Mulchahey, *"First the Bow Is Bent"*; and Jordan, *"Summa's Reform of Moral Teaching."*

33. For understanding *sacra doctrina*, Gerald Van Ackeren, *Sacra Doctrina. The Subject of the First Question of the Summa Theologica of St. Thomas Aquinas* (Rome: Catholic Book Agency, 1952); Weisheipl, "Meaning of *Sacra Doctrina*"; and Mark F. Johnson, "The Sapiential Character of the First Article of the *Summa theologiae*," in *Philosophy and the God of Abraham. Essays in Memory of James A. Weisheipl*, R. James Long, ed. (Toronto: PIMS, 1991), 85–98.

34. *De Trinitate*, q. 5.4 corp. For more on natural *theologia* (= *metaphysica/divina scientia*), see q. 5.1.

35. E.g., Ia, q. 1.7, sed contra. See also the discussion in IIaIIae, q. 1.5, where he uses *theologia* in ad 2.

36. See the discussion of the three senses of *scientia* in Thomas's commentary on Aristotle's *Posterior Analytics*: *In I. Post. Anal.*, c. 28, lect. 41.

37. The structure is set out by Weisheipl, "Meaning of *Sacra Doctrina*," 64–89.

38. Thomas does not introduce the technical term *supernaturalis* in q. 1.1, but this is obviously what he is talking about. The evolution of the distinction between what pertains to nature (*naturalis*) and what goes beyond it in terms of contact with God's own life (*supernaturalis*) was an important aspect of the scholastic effort of the late twelfth though mid-thirteenth centuries. Thomas uses *supernaturalis* and its equivalents about 314 times across his works (115 uses in the *Summa*).

39. Etienne Gilson, *The Philosopher and Theology* (New York: Random House, 1962), 98.

40. In his study of the necessity of *sacra doctrina* for salvation, Bruce D. Marshall notes a text from Thomas's *Sermons on the Apostles' Creed* in which he says that none of the ancient philosophers before Christ knew as much "as one old woman [*vetula*] knows by faith after Christ's coming." See Marshall, "*Quid scit Una Uetula*. Aquinas on the Nature of Theology," in *The Theology of Thomas Aquinas*, Rik Van Nieuwenhove and Joseph Wawrykow, eds. (Notre Dame: University of Notre Dame Press, 2005), 1–35.

41. On *sacra doctrina* and sanctification, Fáinche Ryan, *Formation in Holiness. Thomas Aquinas on "Sacra doctrina"* (Leuven: Peeters, 2007).

42. Two of the major difficulties were the following: (1) How can a discipline that deals with contingent historical facts become universal abstract knowledge? and (2) If science demands both evidence and certitude, where is the evidence in the case of faith? On the scientific nature of theology in the thirteenth century, M.-D. Chenu, *La théologie comme science au XIIIe siècle*, 3rd ed. (Paris: Vrin, 1957); Ulrich Köpf, *Die Anfänge der theologischen Wissenschaftstheorie im 13. Jahrhundert* (Tübingen: Siebeck, 1974); and the essays in *What Is "Theology" in the Middle Ages?*, Mikolaj Olszewski, ed. (Münster: Aschendorff, 2007. Archa Verbi. Subsidia 1).

43. On Thomas's dependence on Aristotle's notion of *scientia* from the *Posterior Analytics*, Jenkins, *Knowledge and Faith in Thomas Aquinas*, especially pt. 1.

44. Aristotle considers metaphysics as wisdom in *Metaphyics* 1.1–2 (981b–983a), and he discusses the difference between practical and philosophical wisdom in *Nicomachean Ethics* 6.3–8 (1139b–1142a).

45. B. Montagnes, "Les deux fonctions de la sagesse: ordonner et juger," *Revue des sciences philosophiques et théologiques* 53 (1969): 675–86.

46. Conley, *Theology of Wisdom*, 38–47, 81–89, and 121–30.

47. See, e.g., IaIIae, q. 66.5; IIIa, q. 59.2 and 4.

48. On *sapientia* as ordering to the proper end, see IaIIae, q. 102.1, and IIaIIae, q. 19.7.

49. Thomas's views on *sapientia* appear throughout the *STh* and his other works—theological wisdom, which is both infused and acquired, is discussed in Ia, q. 1.6, and IIaIIae, q. 19.7; see also *SCG* I.1–2, II.4 and 24, and III.77. Philosophical *sapientia* is treated in the *Sententia super Metaphysicam* I.1.31–35, and in IaIIae, q. 57.2. *Sapientia* as the gift of the Holy Spirit is discussed in *In III Sent.*, d. 34, q. 1.2, and d. 35, q. 2.1, as well as in his *In Isaiam*, cap. 11. It appears in several places in the *Summa*: in the general treatment of the gifts (IaIIae, q. 68.4), and specifically in the treatment of the gift of *sapientia* in IIaIIae, q. 45.1–6 (see also q. 8.6). Also important for Thomas's understanding of *sapientia* are *In I Sent.*, prol., and passages in his Pauline commentaries, such as *In I Cor.* 1:17–31, lect. 3–4; *In I Cor.* 2:1–16, lect. 1–3; and *In Col.* 2:2–3, lect. 1.

50. All three forms of wisdom are primarily intellectual virtues, though they have an intimate relation to the will and affectivity not found in pure *scientia*; see Conley, *Theology of Wisdom*, 45–46, 86–88, 113–21, and 130–32.

51. Weisheipl, "Meaning of *Sacra Doctrina*," 75, summarizes, "[T]he definition of *sacra doctrina* is simply wisdom (art. 6), about God (art. 7) in faith, derived from divine revelation (art. 1)." Wisdom is the goal of all Thomas's writings, as we can see from texts like *SCG* I.2 ("Quae sit hoc opera auctoris intentio"), which begins, "Among all human pursuits the pursuit of wisdom is more perfect, more sublime, more useful, and more pleasing." The basis for the position of wisdom is summarized in Thomas's *In I Cor.* 1:17–25, lect. 3: "Wisdom is the knowledge of divine things and so belongs to contemplation."

52. Thomas reflected on the role of reason and rational argument in sacred teaching in a number of other places: e.g., Ia, q. 32.1; Ia, q. 46.2; *SCG* I.2–3, 8–9; *De Trinitate*, q. 2.3; and *Quod.* IV, q. 9.3.

53. *De Trinitate*, q. 2.3, ad 5.

54. Thomas's role as a scriptural interpreter is studied in Wilhelmus G. B. M. Valkenberg, *Words of the Living God. Place and Function of Holy Scripture in the Theology of Thomas Aquinas* (Leuven: Peeters, 2000); and Thomas Prügl, "Thomas Aquinas as Interpreter of Scripture," in *Theology of Thomas Aquinas*, 386–415.

55. On the apophatic nature of both sapiential theology and the gift of wisdom, Conley, *Theology of Wisdom*, 104, 132–37, and 142–43.

56. Thomas has further reflections on the relation between reading the Bible and the construction of *sacra doctrina* in IIaIIae, q. 1.9. Other explorations of Thomas's hermeneutical theory include *De pot.* q. 4.1, and *Quod.* VII, q. 6.1–3.

57. Ghislain Lafont, *Structures et méthode dans la Somme Théologique de Saint Thomas d'Aquin* (Paris: Desclée, 1961), 34, says, "[T]he problem of the plan of the *Summa*, apparently so clear, is in reality complex." For a recent survey, Brian V. Johnstone, "The Debate on the Structure of the *Summa theologiae* of St. Thomas Aquinas: From Chenu (1939) to Metz (1998)," in *Aquinas as Authority*, Paul van Geest, Harm Goris, and Carlo Leget, eds. (Leuven: Peeters, 2002), 187–200.

58. Thomas F. O'Meara, *Thomas Aquinas. Theologian* (Notre Dame: University of Notre Dame Press, 1997), 53–68.

59. The structure of the *Summa* is both linear, or diachronic, as well as synchronic in the sense that Thomas always keeps the meaning of the whole in mind. As Liam G. Walsh observes, " [Thomas] does not pass from one thing to another. He is looking at everything all of the time, but in a perspective that moves gradually from the more

abstract and universal to the more particular." Walsh, "Sacraments," in *Theology of Thomas Aquinas*, 327.

60. Lonergan, "Future of Thomism," 46.

61. M.-D. Chenu, "Le plan de la Somme théologique de saint Thomas," *Revue thomiste* 47 (1939): 93–107, later incorporated in his *Toward Understanding St. Thomas* (Chicago: Regnery, 1964), 310–18.

62. Thomas refers to the *exitus-reditus* paradigm in *In I Sent.*, d. 2, div. textus; and d. 14, q. 2.2, sol.; as well as in *In II. Sent.*, prol.

63. Among the alternative suggestions, see André Hayen, *St. Thomas et la vie de l'église* (Louvain: Publications Universitaires, 1952), especially 77–100; Albert Patfoort, *La Somme de Saint Thomas et la logique du dessein de Dieu* (Saint-Maur: Éditions Parole et Silence, 1998); and Rudi Te Velde, *Aquinas on God. The "Divine Science" of the Summa Theologiae* (Burlington, VT: Ashgate, 2006), chap. 1.

64. *In I Sent.*, d. 14, q. 2.2, sol.

65. Thomas discusses both the immanent *circulus* of the Trinitarian processions and the external "processio in exteriorem naturam" in *De pot.* q. 9.9, corp.

66. E.g., *SCG* I.9; II.1; III.1; and IV.1; as well as the argument advanced in Torrell, *Saint Thomas Aquinas*, 1:107–16.

67. The triple pattern is part of the structure of the work and appears in such texts as *De divinis nominibus* 1.5. For Thomas's comment on this passage, see his *In Librum De divinis nominibus* (Turin: Marietti, 1950), cap. I, lect. 3, ## 79–95 (pp. 27–29).

68. Max Secklar, *Das Heil in der Geschichte. Geschichtstheologisches Denken bei Thomas von Aquin* (Munich: Kösel Verlag, 1964), 46, puts it as follows: "It [the schema of the *Summa*] signifies nothing else but a total and self-consistent structure of events, or, as we might say now, Aquinas's theological design is based on a formula open to history and therefore enabling

statements about history as meaningful. As a plan of the perspective, it is as much a source of historical understanding as an ordering of theological understanding: it defines the *ordo disciplinae*, because it had already defined the *ordo rerum*." See also Yves Congar, "Le moment 'économique' et le moment 'ontologique' dans la Sacra Doctrina (Révélation, Théologie, Somme Théologique)," in *Mélanges offerts à M.-D. Chenu* (Paris: Bibliothéque Thomiste, 1967), 135–87.

69. On the argument from fittingness, Gilbert Narcisse, *Les raisons de Dieu: Argument de convenience et esthétique théologique selon saint Thomas d'Aquin et Hans Urs von Balthasar* (Fribourg: Éditions universitaires, 1997).

70. The reference to our resurrection in this passage led Johnstone, "Debate on the Structure of the *Summa*," 195–98, to emphasize how Christ's Resurrection (e.g., IIIa, qq. 53–56) functions as a paradigm for Thomas's structuring of sacred history in the *Summa*.

CHAPTER 3   A Tour of the *Summa theologiae*

1. For an analysis of qq. 1–26, Te Velde, *Aquinas on God*.

2. Contrasting evaluations of the five ways can be found in Edward Sillem, *Ways of Thinking about God. Thomas Aquinas and the Modern Mind* (New York: Sheed and Ward, 1961), who defends a reworked version of the five ways, and Anthony Kenny, *The Five Ways. St. Thomas Aquinas's Proofs for God's Existence* (New York: Shocken Books, 1969), who subjects the ways to a strong critique.

3. In *SCG* I.13 Thomas gives a longer and somewhat different version of the five ways more directly based on Aristotle.

4. Jean-Luc Marion, "Thomas Aquinas and Onto-theology," in *Mystics. Presence and Aporia*, Michael Kessler and Christian Sheppard, eds. (Chicago: University of Chicago Press, 2003), 38–74.

5. Etienne Gilson, *Being and Some Philosophers*, 2nd ed. (Toronto: PIMS, 1949).

6. For a succinct presentation, John F. Wipple, "Being," in *The Oxford Handbook of Aquinas*, Brian Davies and Eleonore Stump, eds. (New York: Oxford University Press, 2012), 77–84.

7. David Burrell, *Aquinas. God & Action* (Notre Dame: University of Notre Dame Press, 1979).

8. Te Velde, *Aquinas on God*, 77–85.

9. David Burrell, *Analogy and Philosophical Language* (New Haven: Yale University Press, 1973), puts Aquinas's teaching in historical context.

10. Gilles Emery, *Trinity in Aquinas* (Ann Arbor, MI: Sapientia Press, 2003).

11. See David Burrell, *Freedom and Creation in Three Traditions* (Notre Dame: University of Notre Dame Press, 1993).

12. My understanding of Thomas's teaching on creation and the role of Aristotelian and Platonic elements in it owes much to Joseph de Finance, *Être et Agir dans la Philosophie de Saint Thomas*, 2nd ed. (Rome: Librarie Éditrice de l'Université Grégorienne, 1960).

13. On humanity as made in the image of the Trinitarian God, D. Juvenal Merriel, *To the Image of the Trinity. A Study in the Development of Aquinas' Teaching* (Toronto: PIMS, 1990).

14. The question of the so-called natural desire for God, often misunderstood in later Thomist tradition, was clarified by Henri de Lubac, *The Mystery of the Supernatural* (New York: Herder and Herder, 1967); see also William R. O'Connor, *The Natural Desire for God* (Milwaukee: Marquette University Press, 1948).

15. Anton C. Pegis, *At the Origins of the Thomistic Notion of Man* (New York: Macmillan, 1963), pts. 2 and 4.

16. There is a multiauthor introduction to Thomas's moral theology in *The Ethics of Aquinas*, Stephen J. Pope, ed. (Washington, DC: Georgetown University Press, 2002). See also *Oxford Handbook of Aquinas*, pt. 4.

17. An analysis of the IaIIae can found in Brian Davies, *The Thought of Thomas Aquinas* (New York: Oxford University Press, 1992), chaps. 12 and 13 (pp. 207–73).

18. Bernard Lonergan, *Grace and Freedom. Operative Grace in the Thought of St. Thomas Aquinas* (New York: Herder & Herder, 1971).

19. For an overview, Joseph Wawrykow, "The Theological Virtues," in *Oxford Handbook of Aquinas*, 287–307.

20. On the importance of friendship in Aquinas, Turner, *Thomas Aquinas*, chap. 5 (145–68); and Jean-Pierre Torrell, *Christ and Spirituality in St. Thomas Aquinas* (Washington, DC: Catholic University Press, 2011), chap. 3.

21. For a Thomistically inspired account, Josef Pieper, *The Four Cardinal Virtues: Prudence, Justice, Fortitude, and Temperance* (Notre Dame: University of Notre Dame Press, 1966).

22. For Thomas's Christology and its context, Corey L. Barnes, *Christ's Two Wills in Scholastic Thought. The Christology of Aquinas in Its Historical Context* (Toronto: PIMS, 2012), as well as Joseph Wawrykow, "Hypostatic Union," in *Theology of Thomas Aquinas*, 222–51.

23. On the structure of Thomas's Christology, John F. Boyle, "The Twofold Division of St. Thomas's Christology in the *Tertia Pars*," *Thomist* 60 (2010): 439–47.

24. For an introduction, Walsh, "Sacraments," 326–64.

25. Here Thomas does not use his succinct formulation of sacramental causality found in *De ver.* q. 27.4, ad 13; and q. 28.2, ad 12: "sacraments cause by signifying" (*sacramenta significando causant*).

26. Walsh, "Sacraments," 335.

CHAPTER 4 The Tides of Thomism, 1275–1850

1. On the notion of creative misreadings, Pierre Hadot, *Philosophy as a Way of Life* (Oxford: Blackwell, 1995), chap. 2.

2. The last attempt at a general history was Karl Werner, *Der heilige Thomas von Aquin. Vol. III. Geschichte des Thomismus* (Regensburg: Manz, 1859). Many brief surveys exist, e.g., J. A. Weisheipl, "Thomism," in *The New Catholic Encyclopedia* (New York: Macmillan, 2003), 14:40–52.

3. For an introduction, Martin Grabmann, "History of the Theological *Summa*. Its Commentators," in *Introduction to the Theological Summa of St. Thomas* (St. Louis: B. Herder, 1930), 43–59.

4. Lawrence A. Kennedy, *A Catalogue of Thomists, 1270–1900* (Houston: Center for Thomistic Studies, 1987).

5. For this distinction, Romanus Cessario, *A Short History of Thomism* (Washington, DC: Catholic University Press, 2005); a more flexible view is found in Torrell, *Aquinas's* Summa, "The *Summa* through History" and "The *Summa* in the Twentieth Century."

6. These two ways of reading Thomas on the relation of theology and philosophy are analyzed in Géry Prouvost, *Thomas d'Aquin et les thomismes* (Paris: Les Éditions du Cerf, 2007), chap. 1.

7. Henri de Lubac, *At the Service of the Church* (San Francisco: Ignatius Press, 1993), 144.

8. Gerald Vann, *St. Thomas Aquinas* (New York: Benzinger Brothers, 1947), 71.

9. The Roman Provincial Chapter of Perugia in 1308 forbade the friars substituting the *Summa* for the Lombard's *Sentences* (Mulchahey, *"First the Bow Is Bent,"* 155–56, 161). The Dominican Order did legislate that the *Sentences* be taught along with certain "articles" of the teaching of Thomas, mostly taken from the *Summa*.

10. The Paris Condemnation is document 473 in H. Denifle and A. Chatelain, *Chartularium Universitatis Parisiensis*, vol. 1 (Paris, 1889), 543–58. The Oxford Condemnation follows as document 474 (558–60).

11. Etienne Gilson, *History of Christian Philosophy in the Middle Ages* (New York: Random House, 1955), 408.

12. Alain de Libera, *Penser du moyen âge* (Paris: Seuil, 1993).

13. Luca Bianchi, "1277: A Turning Point in Medieval Philosophy?," in *Was ist Philosophie im Mittelalter?*, Jan A. Aertsen and Andreas Speer, eds. (Berlin: Walter de Gruyter, 1998), 90–110.

14. For an introduction, John F. Wippel, "The Condemnations of 1270 and 1277 at Paris," *Journal of Medieval and Renaissance Studies* 7 (1977): 169–201. More detail can be found in Roland Hissette, *Enquête sur les 219 articles condemnés à Paris le 7 mars 1277* (Louvain: Université Louvain, 1977); and the papers in *Nach der Verurteilung von 1277. Philosophie und Theologie an der Universität Paris im letzten Viertel des 13. Jahrhunderts*, Jan A. Aertsen, Kent Emery, Jr., and Andreas Speer, eds. (Berlin: Walter de Gruyter, 2001).

15. The Dominicans mustered their forces to prevent a formal condemnation of Thomas. A story that seems worthy of credence is that the aged Albert the Great came to Paris in 1276 or 1277 to defend his former student.

16. The Dominican legislation is found in Maur Burbach, "Early Dominican and Franciscan Legislation Regarding St. Thomas," *Mediaeval Studies* 4 (1942): 139–58.

17. The respondents to William de la Mare, as well as other early followers of Thomas, such as the English Dominican Thomas Sutton, the French Bernard of Trilia, and the Belgian Giles of Lessines, are studied by Frederick J. Roensch, *Early Thomistic School* (Dubuque, IA: Priory Press, 1964). See also J.-P. Torrell, "Le savoir théologique

chez les premiers Thomistes," in his *Recherches Thoma-siennes. Études revues et augmentées* (Paris: Vrin, 2000), 158–76.

18. The five *correctoria* defending Thomas include the *Correctorium corruptorii Quare*, probably written by Richard Knapwell ca. 1280–83; the *Correctorium Sciendum*, an English work of ca. 1283, possibly by Robert Orford; the *Correctorium Circa* by John Quidort of Paris, written about 1283–84; the *Correctorium Quaestione*, most likely the work of the Englishman William of Macclesfield in 1284; and the *Apologeticum veritatis* by the Italian Rambert di'Primadizza, written at Paris ca. 1286–88.

19. Mark D. Jordan, "The Controversy of the *Correctoria* and the Limits of Metaphysics," *Speculum* 57 (1982): 292–314; and Maarten J. F. M. Hoenen, "Being and Thinking in the 'Correctorium fratris Thomae' and the 'Correctorium corruptorii Quare,'" in *Nach der Verurteilung von 1277*, 413–35.

20. On John of Freiburg's *Summa Confessorum* (ca. 1298), L. E. Boyle, "The *Summa Confessorum* of John of Freiburg and the Popularization of the Moral Teaching of St. Thomas and Some of His Contemporaries," in *St. Thomas Aquinas, 1274–1294. Commemorative Studies*, 2 vols. (Toronto: PIMS, 1974), 2:245–68.

21. J. N. Hillgarth, "Who Read Thomas Aquinas?", in *The Gilson Lectures on Thomas Aquinas*, James P. Reilly, ed. (Toronto: PIMS, 2002), 46–72.

22. For an introduction, Richard Cross, *Duns Scotus* (New York: Oxford University Press, 1999). Because of Scotus's early death, his major writings are versions of his commentaries on the Lombard's *Sentences* given at Oxford and Paris. The Oxford *Lectura* seems to date from 1298–99, while the longer *Ordinatio* and *Reportatio Parisiensia* reflect his teaching in Paris (1301–4).

23. See Cross, *Duns Scotus*, chap. 1; Stephen F. Brown, "Scotus's Method in Theology," in *Via Scoti. Methodologica ad mentem Joannis Duns Scoti*, Leonardo Sileo, ed. (Rome: Edizioni Antonianum, 1995), 229–43; and Oleg Bychkov, "The Nature of Theology in Duns Scotus and His Franciscan Predecessors," *Franciscan Studies* 66 (2008): 5–62.

24. This Prologue takes up the first volume of the critical edition, *Iohannis Duns Scoti Opera Omnia* (Rome: Vatican Press, 1950–).

25. *Reportatio Parisiensia*, Liber Tertius, d. 24, can be found in *Joannis Duns Scoti Opera Omnia* (Paris: L. Vivès, 1894), 13:446–59.

26. *Ordinatio*, Prol., Pars 1, q. unica, n. 79, cites and rebuts *STh* Ia, q. 1.1, ad 2. See also Pars 5, qq. 1–2, n. 313.

27. See Bychkov, "Nature of Theology in Duns Scotus," 44–62.

28. The surviving parts of the *Opus Tripartitum* are in *Meister Eckhart. Die deutschen und lateinischen Werke* (Stuttgart: Kohlhammer, 1936–), *Die lateinischen Werke*, vols. 1–3. I count 122 explicit references to Thomas in these volumes, while the indices list no fewer than 516 direct or indirect uses of the *Prima Pars*, 202 of the IaIIa, 75 of the IIaIIae, and 38 of the IIIa.

29. For an introduction, Alain de Libera, *La mystique rhénane. D'Albert le Grand à Maître Eckhart* (Paris: Éditions du Seuil, 1994). The texts of these Dominicans are being edited in the *Corpus Philosophorum Teutonicorum Medii Aevi*.

30. For aspects of the relation of Thomas and Eckhart, Bernard McGinn, *The Mystical Thought of Meister Eckhart* (New York: Crossroad, 2001), which also contains references to further literature.

31. On the contrast between Eckhart's ethical thought and that of Thomas, John M. Connolly, *Living Without Why: Meister Eckhart's Critique of the Medieval Concept of Will* (Oxford: Oxford University Press, 2014).

32. For an overview, Thomas Tyn, "Prochoris und Demetrios Kydones. Der Byzantinische Thomismus des 14. Jahrhunderts," in *Thomas von Aquino. Interpretation und Rezeption*, Willehad Paul Eckert, ed. (Mainz: Matthias-Grünewald-Verlag, 1974), 837–912.

33. John Monfasani, *Bessarion Scholasticus. A Study of Cardinal Bessarion's Latin Library* (Turnhout: Brepols, 2011), "The Thomism of Cardinal Bessarion" (61–81).

34. For a sketch of medieval Jewish uses of Thomas, Giuseppe Sermonetta, "Per una storia del Tomismo Ebraico," in *Tommaso d'Aquino nella storia del pensiero. Vol. II. Dal Medioevo al Oggi* (Naples: Edizioni Domeniche Italiane, 1974), 354–59.

35. Lonergan, "Future of Thomism," 53.

36. Paul J. Griffiths, *Religious Reading* (New York: Oxford University Press, 1999), 77–97.

37. *Johannis Capreoli Defensiones Theologiae Divi Thomae Aquinatis*, Ceslaus Paban and Thomas Pègues, eds., 7 vols. (repr., Frankfurt am Main: Minerva, 1967), 1:1.

38. *Defensiones* Q. 1, a. 1, 5th conclusion (1:4).

39. On this development, Yves Congar, *A History of Theology* (Garden City, NY: Doubleday, 1968), 154–62.

40. Harm Goris, "Thomism in Fifteenth-Century Germany," in *Aquinas as Authority*, 1–24; as well as Erich Höhn, "Köln als der Ort der ersten Kommentare zur 'Summa theologiae' des Thomas von Aquin," in *Thomas von Aquino. Interpretation und Rezeption*, 641–55.

41. The best account is Paul Oskar Kristeller, *Le Thomisme et la pensée Italienne de la Renaissance* (Montreal: Institut d'Études Médiévales-Vrin, 1967).

42. John O'Malley, "Some Renaissance Panegyrics of Aquinas," *Renaissance Quarterly* 27 (1974): 174–92.

43. Edward P. Mahoney, "St. Thomas and the School of Padua at the End of the Fifteenth Century," *Thomas and*

Bonaventure. *Proceedings of the American Catholic Philo-sophical Society* 48 (1974): 277–85.

44. On Ficino and Thomas, Kristeller, *Thomisme et la pensée Italienne*, 93–101. For more detail, Ardis B. Collins, *The Sacred Is Secular: Platonism and Thomism in Marsilio Ficino's Platonic Theology* (The Hague: Nijhoff, 1974).

45. On the famous nondisputation, S. A. Farmer, *Syncretism in the West: Pico's 900 Theses (1486). The Evolution of Traditional Religious and Philosophical Systems* (Tempe, AZ: Medieval and Renaissance Texts and Studies, 1998), where the Thomist theses can be found on 218–31 (see also 47–49, 422, on Pico's anti-Thomism).

46. The commentaries of this period are briefly discussed in the histories of Thomism by Cessario, Torrell, et al.; see also Philippe Lécrivain, "La Somme théologique de Thomas d'Aquin aux XVIe–XVIIIe siècles," *Recherches de science religieuse* 91 (2003): 397–427.

47. On Cajetan, Jared Wicks, "Thomism between Renaissance and Reformation: The Case of Cajetan," *Archiv für Reformationsgeschichte* 68 (1977): 9–32; and Martin Grabmann, "Die Stellung des Kardinal Cajetan in der Geschichte des Thomismus und der Thomistenschule," in *Mittelalterliches Geistesleben*, Martin Grabmann, ed., 3 vols. (repr., Hildesheim: G. Olms, 1984), 2:602–13.

48. Henri De Lubac, *Augustinianism and Modern Theology* (New York: Crossroad, 2000), chap. 5.

49. Leonard Kennedy, "Thomism at the University of Sala-manca in the Sixteenth Century: The Doctrine of Exis-tence," in *Tommaso d'Aquino nella storia del pensiero*, 2:254–58.

50. *D. Martin Luthers Werke* (Weimar: Böhlaus, 1899), 15:184 (32–33).

51. Denis R. Janz, "Thomas Aquinas, Martin Luther, and the Origins of the Protestant Reformation," in *Philosophy and the God of Abraham*, 71–83; and David C. Steinmetz,

"Luther among the Anti-Thomists," in *Luther in Context* (Bloomington: Indiana University Press, 1986), chap. 5.

52. *D. Martin Luthers Werke* (Weimar: Böhlaus, 1888), 6:508 (11–12).

53. Karl-Heinz zur Mühlen, "On the Critical Reception of the Thought of Thomas Aquinas in the Theology of Martin Luther," in *Aquinas as Authority*, 65–86.

54. Pesch has written extensively on Thomas and Luther in German. In English, see Otto H. Pesch, "Existential and Sapiential Theology—The Theological Confrontation between Luther and Thomas Aquinas," in *Catholic Scholars Dialogue with Luther*, Jared Wicks, ed. (Chicago: Loyola University Press, 1970), 59–81; and *The God Question in Thomas Aquinas and Martin Luther* (Philadelphia: Fortress Press, 1972).

55. Pesch, "Existential and Sapiential Theology," 76.

56. For knowledge of Thomas and the *Summa* in Protestant England, John K. Ryan, *The Reputation of St. Thomas Aquinas among English Protestant Thinkers of the Seventeenth Century* (Washington, DC: Catholic University Press, 1948).

57. On Trent and its significance, John O'Malley, *Trent. What Happened at the Council* (Cambridge, MA: Belknap, 2013).

58. On these discussions, Hubert Jedin, *A History of the Council of Trent* (St. Louis: B. Herder, 1961), 2:286–96, and 387–88.

59. A single example must suffice. In the early debates over original sin directed against Luther, the Thomist party introduced Thomas's distinction (IaIIae, q. 82.3) that baptism forgives the formal element of the sin, but that the material element called "concupiscence" remains. This language was approved in the draft, but not included in the final decree.

60. Bañez's *Scholastica commentaria in primam partem Angelici Doctoris* was first published in Salamanca in 1584.

61. Matthias Lu, "La diffusione delle Opere di Tommaso d'Aquino in Cina," in *Tommaso d'Aquino nella storia del pensiero*, 2:367–74.

62. Suarez's metaphysics is set forth in his *Disputationes Metaphysicae* of 1597, which were widely read and constituted the major link between medieval philosophy and the new philosophy of the seventeenth century. On Suarez's metaphysics and its difference from Thomas, Gilson, *Being and Some Philosophers*, 96–107; and John P. Doyle, *Collected Studies on Francisco Suarez, S. J. (1548–1617)* (Leuven: Leuven University Press, 2010).

63. Molina's teaching on "middle knowledge" is available in English, *Luis de Molina. On Divine Foreknowledge. Part IV of the "Concordia,"* trans. Alfred J. Freddoso (Ithaca: Cornell University Press, 1988).

64. For an English translation, *The Gifts of the Holy Spirit by John of St. Thomas* (New York: Sheed and Ward, 1951).

65. The original edition of the *Collegii Salmanticensis... Cursus Theologicus Summam theologicam Angelici Doctoris D. Thomae complectens* was published in ten volumes. The most accessible edition is the twenty-volume Paris edition of 1870–83.

66. Among the foremost of these commentators are John Gonet (d. 1681), who issued a number of commentaries and defenses of Thomas late in the seventeenth century, and the Dominican Charles René Billuart (d. 1757), who published an eighteen-volume commentary on the *Summa* between 1746 and 1751.

67. *The Letters and Diaries of John Henry Newman*, Charles Stephen Dessain, ed. (London: Nelson, 1961), 11:279. See also the comments on "the prevalent depreciation of St. Thomas" found in another letter in the same volume (pp. 303–5).

1. James Hennesey, "Leo XIII's Thomistic Revival: A Political and Philosophical Event," in *Celebrating the Medieval Heritage. A Colloquy on the Thought of Aquinas and Bonaventure*, David Tracy, ed., *Journal of Religion* suppl. 58 [1978]: S185–97.

2. On nineteenth-century Catholic theology, Mark Schoof, *A Survey of Catholic Theology 1800–1970* (Eugene, OR: Wipf & Stock, 2008); and especially Gerald A. McCool, *Nineteenth-Century Scholasticism. The Search for a Unitary Method* (New York: Fordham University Press, 1989).

3. Many of the documents, such as the papal encyclical *Aeterni Patris* of 1879, speak of the renewal of "scholastic philosophy" (*philosophia scholastica*); hence the term "Neoscholasticism" is often used to describe this movement in modern Catholic thought. In practice, however, Thomas Aquinas was seen as *the* Neoscholastic author. All other scholastics, including such distinctive thinkers as Bonaventure, were reduced to agreeing with Thomas. Hence, the terms "Neoscholasticism" and "Neothomism" can be used interchangeably.

4. Along with McCool's book, see James A. Weisheipl, "The Revival of Thomism as a Christian Philosophy," in *New Themes in Christian Philosophy*, Ralph McInerny, ed. (Notre Dame: University of Notre Dame Press, 1968), 164–85; and Leonard E. Boyle, "A Remembrance of Pope Leo XIII: The Encyclical *Aeterni Patris*," in *One Hundred Years of Thomism. Aeterni Patris and Afterwards*, Victor B. Brezik, ed. (Houston: Center for Thomistic Studies, 1981), 7–22.

5. On the relation of *Dei Filius* to Neoscholasticism, McCool, *Nineteenth-Century Scholasticism*, 216–26.

6. Hennesy, "Leo XIII's Thomistic Revival," S190.

7. Ibid., S192, quoting the historian of nineteenth-century theology Edgar Hocedez.

8. On Liberatore and Kleutgen, McCool, *Nineteenth-Century Scholasticism*, chaps. 7–9.

9. Mark Jordan, *Rewritten Theology. Aquinas after His Readers* (Oxford: Blackwell, 2006), chap. 1, especially 5–12.

10. For reflections on the reasons for the academic success (and limitations) of Neothomism, Marcia L. Colish, "St. Thomas Aquinas in Historical Perspective: The Modern Period," *Church History* 44 (1975): 13–16.

11. Robert F. McNamara, *The American College in Rome, 1855–1955* (Rochester, NY: Christopher Press, 1956), 243.

12. Josiah Royce, "Pope Leo's Philosophical Movement: Its Relation to Modern Thought," *Tablet* 102 (August 15, 1903), 260–62.

13. An account of the editions of Thomas's *Opera omnia*, including the beginnings of the Leonine edition, can be found in Louis-Jacques Bataillon, "Le Edizioni di *Opera Omnia* degli Scolastici e l'Edizione Leonina," in *Gli studi di Filosofia medievale fra Ottocento e Novecento*, Ruedi Imbach and Alfonso Maierù, eds. (Rome: Edizioni di Storia et Letteratura, 1991), 141–54.

14. On the Leonine Commission, see also James P. Reilly, Jr., "The Leonine Commission and the Seventh Centenary of St. Thomas Aquinas," in *Thomas and Bonaventure. Proceedings of the American Catholic Philosophical Association* 48 (1974): 286–94.

15. Bataillon, "Le Edizioni di *Opera Omnia*," 154.

16. For historical surveys, Alec Vidler, *A Variety of Catholic Modernists* (Cambridge: Cambridge University Press, 1970); and Marvin R. O'Connell, *Critics on Trial. An Introduction to the Catholic Modernist Crisis* (Washington, DC: Catholic University Press, 1994). On the relation of Modernism to Neothomism, Thomas J. A. Hartley,

Thomistic Revival and the Modernist Era (Toronto: St. Michael's College, 1971).

17. Late in the encyclical Pius summarizes his view: "[T]here is no surer sign that a man is tending to Modernism than when he begins to show his dislike for the scholastic method." See *Pascendi Dominici Gregis*, as translated in *The Program of Modernism. A Reply to the Encyclical of Pius X* (New York: G.P. Putnam, 1908), 222.

18. The Italian original, *Il Programma dei Modernisti*, was published in 1907; the English version, translated by Tyrrell, appeared in 1908. The quotation is from *Program of Modernism*, 6.

19. The decree can be found in *Heinrich Denzinger. Compendium of Creeds, Definitions, and Declarations on Matters of Faith and Morals*, Peter Hünermann, ed., bilingual 43rd ed. (San Francisco: Ignatius Press, 2012), nos. 3601–24. The major author of the twenty-four theses was the Jesuit Guido Mattuissi (1852–1925), a student of Cardinal Billot and an opponent of the Suarezians.

20. These quotations from *Humani Generis* are taken from the English translation, *False Trends in Modern Teaching* (London: Catholic Truth Society, 1957), secs. 18 and 31.

21. Torrell, *Aquinas's* Summa, 110–11.

22. Among the surveys of modern Thomism I have found helpful are O'Meara, *Thomas Aquinas*, 167–200; Helen James John, *The Thomist Spectrum* (New York: Fordham University Press, 1966); Gerald McCool, *From Unity to Pluralism. The Internal Evolution of Thomism* (New York: Fordham University Press, 1989); and Fergus Kerr, *After Aquinas. Versions of Thomism* (Oxford: Blackwell, 2002). More briefly, Gerald A. McCool, "Twentieth-Century Scholasticism," in *Celebrating the Medieval Heritage*, S198–221; Brian J. Shanley, "Twentieth-Century Thomisms," in *The Thomist Tradition* (Dordrecht: Kluwer, 2002), 1–20; and J.-P. Torrell, "Situation actuelle des

études thomistes," in *Nouvelles recherches thomasiennes* (Paris: Vrin, 2008), 177–202.

23. Richard Peddicord, *The Sacred Monster of Thomism. An Introduction to the Life and Legacy of Réginald Garrigou-Lagrange, O.P.* (South Bend, IN: St. Augustine's Press, 2005) is a helpful, but perhaps too favorable, presentation.

24. Garrigou-Lagrange at times carried his Thomism to ridiculous lengths, as when he argued on Thomist grounds during World War II that it was a mortal sin for French Catholics to support the Free French Movement of Charles de Gaulle against the Fascist Vichy government! On his political views, Peddicord, *Sacred Monster of Thomism*, 96–100.

25. Chenu, *Toward Understanding St. Thomas*, 68–69.

26. There is an account of the conflict between Garrigou-Lagrange and Chenu in Peddicord, *Sacred Monster of Thomism*, 100–113.

27. There is an English translation of the second edition, *The Mystery of the Supernatural* (New York: Herder and Herder, 1967).

28. John F. Wippel, *Metaphysical Themes in Thomas Aquinas* (Washington, DC: Catholic University Press, 1984); and *The Metaphysical Thought of Thomas Aquinas. From Finite Being to Uncreated Being* (Washington, DC: Catholic University Press, 2000).

29. A short work originally given as a series of lectures at the Angelicum in Rome in 1931 and later appearing in English in 1940 as *Science and Wisdom* provides a sense of Maritain's view of the integrative role of Thomas's wisdom.

30. Gilson wrote an illuminating intellectual autobiography late in life, *Philosopher and Theology*.

31. Ibid., 91.

32. Gilson's view of Christian philosophy and the difficulties involved in extracting a philosophy from Thomas's mostly theological writings are surveyed by John F. Wippel,

"Thomas Aquinas and the Problem of Christian Philosophy," in *Metaphysical Themes in Thomas Aquinas*, 1–33.

33. Gilson, *Philosopher and Theology*, 211.

34. Finance, *Être et Agir dans la Philosophie de Saint Thomas*,
x. The work has not been translated into English.

35. These contributions to Thomist metaphysics are surveyed
in John, *Thomist Spectrum*, chaps. 6–7.

36. Gilson's rejection of what became Transcendental Thomism is evident in his critical remarks about Joseph
Maréchal in *Thomist Realism and the Critique of Knowledge* (San Francisco: Ignatius Press, 1986; French original
1939), chaps. 5–6.

37. A brief survey can be found in W. J. Hill, "Thomism,
Transcendental," *New Catholic Encyclopedia*, 14: 52–57.
More detailed treatments are in John, *Thomist Spectrum*,
pt. 3; and McCool, *From Unity to Pluralism*, chaps. 2–4.

38. For an English translation, *The Intellectualism of Saint
Thomas* (New York: Sheed and Ward, 1935).

39. Ibid., 2.

40. Joseph Maréchal, "A propos du sentiment de presence
chez les profanes et chez les mystiques," *Revue des questions scientifiques* 64–65 (1908–9), later included in vol.
1 of his *Études sur la Psychologie des Mystiques* (Bruges:
Beyaert-Alcan, 1924), 69–179. This was translated as
Studies in the Psychology of the Mystics (London: Burns &
Oates, 1927), 55–145.

41. These quotations are from Maréchal, *Studies in the Psychology of the Mystics*, 61 and 101.

42. Ibid., 135.

43. McCool, *From Unity to Pluralism*, 110.

44. Lonergan, *Grace and Freedom*.

45. The "Verbum" articles appeared in *Theological Studies*
between 1946 and 1949 and were published in book form
as *Verbum. Word and Idea in Aquinas* (Notre Dame: University of Notre Dame Press, 1967).

46. Ibid., 85.

47. Karl Rahner, "The Importance of Thomas Aquinas," in *Faith in a Wintry Season. Conversations and Interviews with Karl Rahner in the Last Years of His Life* (New York: Crossroad, 1990), 47.

48. Ibid., 43.

49. Hans Urs von Balthasar, *Thomas und die Charismatik. Kommentar zu Thomas von Aquin, Summa theologica Quaestiones II II 171–182* (Einsiedeln: Johannes Verlag, 1954).

50. Hans Urs von Balthasar, *Theo-Drama. Theological Dramatic Theory. V: The Last Act* (San Francisco: Ignatius, 1998), 14.

51. Hans Urs von Balthasar, *The Glory of the Lord. A Theological Aesthetics. IV: The Realm of Metaphysics in Antiquity* (San Francisco: Ignatius, 1989), 405.

52. On Vatican II, John O'Malley, *What Happened at Vatican II* (Cambridge, MA: Harvard University Press, 2008).

53. The largest of the collections published for Thomas's centenary was the nine volumes of the *Atti del Congresso Internazionale Tommaso d'Aquino* produced by the Dominicans of Naples and containing 459 articles.

EPILOGUE

1. Fergus Kerr, *After Aquinas*, 207. Along with this survey of recent trends in Thomist studies, Kerr also edited the collection, *Contemplating Aquinas*.

2. *Encyclical Letter "Fides et Ratio" of the Supreme Pontiff John Paul II* (Washington, DC: U.S. Catholic Conference, 1998), sec. 76 (p. 110).

3. Ibid., especially secs. 43–44 (pp. 65–68) titled "The Enduring Originality of the Thought of Thomas Aquinas," and secs. 57–63 (pp. 87–94) on "The Church's Interest in Philosophy."

4. Jean-Pierre Torrell titled the second volume of his summary work on Aquinas *Saint Thomas Aquinas. Spiritual Master* (1996; English version 2003).

5. "Analytical Thomism" was pioneered by Peter Geach and John Haldane, and has been carried forward by scholars like Anthony Kenny, the late Norman Kretzmann, and Eleonore Stump.

6. Among the projections about the future direction of Thomism that merit pondering: W. Norris Clarke, "The Future of Thomism," in *New Themes in Christian Philosophy*, 187–207; Lonergan, "Future of Thomism," 43–53; and Benedict M. Ashley, "Thomism and the Transition from the Classical World-View to Historical-Mindedness," in *The Future of Thomism* (Notre Dame: American Maritain Society, 1992), 109–21.

BIBLIOGRAPHY

I. Translations of the *Summa theologiae*

A. Complete Versions

St. *Thomas Aquinas. Summa theologiae. Latin text and English translation, Introduction, Notes, Appendices and Glossaries.* Published in 61 vols. (1964–81) and available online.

St. *Thomas Aquinas. Summa Theologica.* First published in 22 vols. in New York (1911–25), reprinted in 3 vols. (1947–48), and in 5 vols. by Christian Classics of Westminster, MD (1981).

B. Selections from the *Summa*

Bauerschmidt, Frederick Christian. *Holy Teaching. Introducing the "Summa Theologiae" of St. Thomas Aquinas.* Grand Rapids, MI: Brazos Press, 2005.

Fairweather, A. M., ed. *Nature and Grace. Selections from the "Summa Theologica" of Thomas Aquinas.* Philadelphia: Westminster Press, 1954.

McInerny, Ralph. *Thomas Aquinas. Selected Writings.* New York: Penguin, 1998.

Pegis, Anton C. *Introduction to St. Thomas Aquinas.* New York: Random House, 1948.

II. General Books on Thomas and His Thought

A. Individual Studies

Chenu, M.-D. *Toward Understanding St. Thomas.* Chicago: Regnery, 1964.

Chesterton, G. K. *St. Thomas Aquinas.* London: Sheed and Ward, 1933.

Davies, Brian. *The Thought of Thomas Aquinas.* New York: Oxford University Press, 1992.

Gilson, Etienne. *The Christian Philosophy of St. Thomas Aquinas.* New York: Random House, 1956.

Nichols, Aidan. *Discovering Aquinas. An Introduction to His Life, Work, and Influence.* Grand Rapids, MI: Eerdmans, 2002.

O'Meara, Thomas. F. *Thomas Aquinas. Theologian.* Notre Dame: University of Notre Dame Press, 1997.

Pieper, Josef. *The Silence of St. Thomas. Three Essays.* Chicago: Regnery, 1965.

Torrell, Jean-Pierre. *Saint Thomas Aquinas.* 2 vols. Washington, DC: Catholic University Press, 1996, 2003.

Turner, Denys. *Thomas Aquinas.* New Haven: Yale University Press, 2013.

Weisheipl, James A. *Friar Thomas D'Aquino. His Life, Thought, and Work.* Garden City, NY: Doubleday, 1974.

B. Collections

Davies, Brian and Eleonore Stump, eds. *The Oxford Handbook of Aquinas.* New York: Oxford University Press, 2012.

Kretzmann, Norman and Eleonore Stump, eds. *The Cambridge Companion to Aquinas.* Cambridge: Cambridge University Press, 1993.

Van Nieuwenhove, Rik and Joseph Wawrykow, eds. *The Theology of Thomas Aquinas*. Notre Dame: University of Notre Dame Press, 2005.

III. Particular Studies of Thomas's Thought Relating to the *Summa*

Burrell, David A. *Aquinas. God & Action*. Notre Dame: University of Notre Dame Press, 1979.

Conley, Kieran. *A Theology of Wisdom. A Study in St. Thomas*. Dubuque, IA: Priory Press, 1963.

Emery, Gilles. *Trinity in Aquinas*. Ann Arbor, MI: Sapientia Press, 2003.

Jordan, Mark D. *Rewritten Theology. Aquinas after His Readers*. Oxford: Blackwell, 2006.

Lonergan, Bernard J. *Verbum. Word and Idea in Aquinas*. Notre Dame: University of Notre Dame Press, 1967.

Pegis, Anton C. *At the Origins of the Thomistic Notion of Man*. New York: Macmillan, 1963.

Te Velde, Rudi. *Aquinas on God. The "Divine Science" of the Summa Theologiae*. Burlington, VT: Ashgate, 2006.

Torrell, Jean-Pierre. *Christ and Spirituality in St. Thomas Aquinas*. Washington, DC: Catholic University Press, 2011.

Van Ackeren, Gerald F. *Sacra Doctrina. The Subject of the First Question of the Summa Theologica of St. Thomas Aquinas*. Rome: Catholic Book Agency, 1952.

IV. Histories of Thomism

Kerr, Fergus. *After Aquinas. Versions of Thomism*. Oxford: Blackwell, 2002.

McCool, Gerald A. *From Unity to Pluralism. The Internal Evolution of Thomism*. New York: Fordham University Press, 1989.

Torrell, Jean-Pierre. *Aquinas's* Summa. *Background, Structure, & Reception*. Washington, DC: Catholic University Press, 2005.

v. Online Resources

For finding Thomas's texts: www.corpusthomisticum.org
For links to Thomas research, the Grand Portal Thomas d'Aquin: www.thomas-d-aquin.com

NAME AND TITLE INDEX

Abelard, Peter, 13, 15
Aeterni Patris 169–71, 173–74,
  180, 182, 187, 211
Against the Errors of the Greeks
  (Contra errores graecorum), 29
Albert the Great, 21- 23, 31–32,
  131, 170
Allodi, Giovanni Maria, 175
Anselm of Canterbury, 9
Antonio de Lucca, 175
Aristotle (The Philosopher),
  4, 10–14, 20–21, 29–33, 35,
  41–42, 49, 56–60, 63, 71, 81,
  83, 90–95, 98–101, 103, 106,
  121–22, 133, 136, 142, 145, 148,
  161, 194, 197, 205
Augustine, 12, 14, 32–33, 42, 56,
  58, 61, 90, 94–95, 99–100,
  106, 109, 113, 124, 157, 191, 195,
  207, 211
Averroes, 31–32, 122, 136, 142

Bandelli, Vincent, 141
Bañez, Domingo, 153, 156–57, 203
Bartholomew of Capua, 43
Bataillon, Louis-Jacques, 176

Bellarmine, Robert, 157
Benedict XV, Pope, 184
Bergson, Henri, 187, 193, 195,
  199, 213
Bernard of Clairvaux, 15, 195
Bertano, Pietro, 153
Bessarion, Cardinal, 136
Biel, Gabriel, 148
Billot, Louis, 169
Blondel, Maurice, 178–79, 182,
  199
Boethius of Dacia, 4, 13, 27, 33,
  41–42, 52, 61
Bonaventure of Bagnorea,
  25–26, 32–33, 38, 90, 120, 124,
  127, 170, 195, 208
Bourret, Stephen, 135
Buglio, Louis, 155
Buonaiuti, Ernesto, 179, 182
Burkhardt, Jacob, 140–41
Busa, Robert, 140

Cajetan, Cardinal (Tommaso
  di Vio), 140, 144–47, 149, 155,
  158, 186–87, 193–94
Calvin, John, 157

Cano, Melchior, 153
Capponi, Seraphino, 153
Capreolus, John, 137–38
Catharinus, Ambrose, 149
Chenu, Marie-Dominique, 68,
    189–92
Chrysostom, John, 34
Clement VIII, Pope, 157
Clement XIV, Pope, 165
*Commentary on Boethius's "De
    hebdomadibus"(Expositio
    super librum Boethii "De
    Hebdomadibus")*, 4, 42
*Commentary on Boethius's "De
    Trinitate"(Expositio super
    librum Boethii "De Trinitate")*,
    13, 27, 42, 61
*Commentary on Isaiah (Expositio
    super Isaiam)*, 22
*Commentary on Job (Expositio
    super Job)*, 28
*Compendium of Theology (Com-
    pendium theologiae)*, 37, 41
Congar, Yves, 190
Crockaert, Peter, 140, 147
Cydones, Demetrios, 136
Cyril of Alexandria, 169

d'Azeglio, Luigi Taparelli, 166
De Finance, Joseph, 197–98
Dei Filius (Pius IX), 167
De Lubac, Henri, 119, 191–92
Denys the Carthusian, 140
Descartes, René, 160–61, 166,
    172, 194–95
Dietrich of Freiburg, 131–33
Dionysius the Areopagite,
    Dionysian corpus, 21–22, 42,
    48, 63, 68, 70, 85, 131
*Disputed Questions on Evil
    (Quaestiones disputatae de
    malo)*, 67

*Disputed Questions on the Power
    of God (Quaestiones disputatae
    de potentia dei)*, 67
*Disputed Questions on Truth
    (Quaestiones disputatae de
    veritate)*, 67
*Disputed Questions on the Virtues
    (Quaestiones disputatae de
    virtutibus)*, 36
Doctoris Angelici (Pius X), 183
Dominic Guzman (Saint Domi-
    nic), 17, 18, 44
Dominici, Giovanni, 134
Duns Scotus, John, 110, 127–30,
    155, 195
Durandus of St. Pourçain, 125,
    138
Durkheim, Emile, 195

Eckhart, Meister, 130–34

Fabro, Cornelio, 198
Ficino, Marsilio, 142–43
Fides et Ratio (John Paul II), 211
Francis of Assisi, 17
Franzelin, J. B., 167
Frederick II, 19–20
Fricia, Nicholas, 36

Gardeil, Ambrose, 187–88
Garrigou-Lagrange, Reginald,
    187–91, 199
Geiger, L.-B., 198
Gerard of Elten, 139
Gibbons, James, Cardinal, 174
Gilbert of Poitiers, 13
Giles of Rome, 123, 127
Gilson, Etienne, 55, 84, 121, 153,
    186, 193, 195–97, 199, 202, 206
Glossa Ordinaria, 12
Godfrey of Fontaines, 127
Golden Chain (Catena Aurea), 29

Gonzales, Zeferino, 167
Gregory I, the Great, Pope, 106
Gregory VII, Pope, 8
Gregory X, Pope, 38
Gregory XIII, Pope, 155
Gregory XVI, Pope, 164
Griffiths, Paul, 137
Grotius, Hugo, 148

Heidegger, Martin, 204, 213
Hennessy, James, 168
Henry of Ghent, 120, 122, 127, 138
Henry of Gorcum, 139
Hermes, Georg, 165
Hillel of Verona, Rabbi, 136
Honecker, Martin, 204
Honorius III, Pope, 44
Humani generis (Pius XII), 184
Humbert of Romans, 18
Hume, David, 160

Ibn Rushd. *See* Averroes
Index Thomisticus, 140
Innocent VIII, Pope, 143
Isidore of Seville, 113

Jehuda ben Daniel Romano, 136
John of Freiburg, 127
John of Sterngassen, 132
John of St. Thomas (John Poinsot), 158, 187–88, 193, 195
John of the Cross, 188, 195
John XXII, Pope, 134
John XXIII, Pope (Giuseppe Angelo Roncalli), 180, 207
John Paul II, Pope, 210–11

Kant, Immanuel, 160, 165, 198, 201–2, 205, 213
Kerr, Fergus, 210
Kilwardby, Robert, 123, 126

Kleutgen, Johannes, 167, 169, 171–73
Knapwell, Richard, 126
Köllin, Konrad, 140
Kraus, Franz, 179
Kuhn, J. E., 165

Laberthonnière, Lucien, 179, 181
Lagrange, Marie-Joseph, 182
Lamentabili (Pius X), 179
Landolph de Aquino (father of Thomas Aquinas), 19
Lanfranc of Bec, 9
Lemius, Joseph, 179
Leo XII, Pope, 164
Leo XIII, Pope (Vincenzo Gioacchino Pecci), 146, 152, 166–71, 173–76, 179, 184, 186–87, 189, 193–94, 196, 206, 208
Lévy-Bruhl, Lucien, 195
Liberatore, Matteo, 169, 171–73
Locke, John, 160, 172
Loisy, Alfred, 178, 181
Lonergan, Bernard, 7, 67, 137, 202–5
Louis IX, 26
Loyola, Ignatius, 154–55
Lumen Ecclesiae (Paul VI), 209
Luther, Martin, 144–45, 147–51

Maimonides, Moses, 86,
Mandonnet, Pierre, 189
Maréchal, Joseph, 200–204
Maritain, Jacques, 186, 193–95, 199, 202, 206
Martin of Paderborn, 167
Mauriac, François, 187
McCool, Gerald, 202
Medina, Bartolomeo de, 153
Mercier, Desiré Joseph, Cardinal, 177, 180–81

Mohler, J. A., 165
Molina, Luis de, 156–57
Murri, Romolo, 179

Napoleon I, 163–64
Napoleon III, 164
Nestorius, 169
Newman, John Henry, 161–62
Nicholas IV, Pope, 126

On Being and Essence (De ente et essentia), 43
On Perfection (De perfectione vitae religiosae), 26
On the Articles of the Faith and the Sacraments of the Church (De articulis fidei et sacramentis ecclesiae), 43, 206
On the Eternity of the World Against the Murmurers (De aeternitate mundi contra murmurantes), 35
On the Unity of the Intellect Against the Averroists (De unitate intellectus contra Averroistas), 35, 43

Pascendi dominici gregis (Pius X), 179–82
Pastor Aeternus (Pius IX), 167
Paul III, Pope, 151
Paul V, Pope, 157
Paul VI, Pope, 209
Pecci, Joseph, 169
Pecham, John, 33, 35, 124, 126
Pesch, Otto Hermann, 150, 212
Peter of Bergamo, 140
Peter Cantor, 15
Peter of Ireland, 20
Peter Lombard, 14–15, 21, 41, 47, 49, 70, 78, 113, 119–20, 126
Philip IV, 158

Pico della Mirandola, Giovanni, 142–43
Pius, IV, Pope, 151
Pius V, Pope, 146, 153–54, 175
Pius VII, Pope, 164, 166
Pius VIII, Pope, 164
Pius IX, Pope, 164, 166, 168
Pius X, Pope, 179–80, 182–84
Pius XI, Pope, 184
Pius XII, Pope, 184–85
Placere nobis (Leo XIII), 175
Plato, 92
Prierias, Sylvester, 149
Pseudo-Dionysius. *See* Dionysius the Areopagite

Quodlibetal Questions (Quaestiones disputatae quodlibetales), 36, 66

Rahner, Karl, 204–05
Reginald of Piperno, 34, 37, 38, 107
Rosmini, Antonio, 172
Royce, Josiah, 174
Rousselot, Pierre, 199–200, 202

Sauer, Josef, 179
Seripando, Girolamo, Cardinal, 152
Siger of Brabant, 32, 35, 43, 90
Silvestri of Ferrara, Francisco, 147
Simeoni, Giovanni, 175
Soto, Domingo de, 148, 153
Spagnoli, Battista (Mantuanus), 141
Studiorum ducem (Pius XI), 184
Suarez, Francisco, 155–56, 158, 161, 166, 183
Suermondt, Constantius, 176

Summa against the Pagans (Summa contra Gentiles), 5, 28, 41, 57, 70, 109, 136, 143, 147, 213
Syllabus of Errors, 166, 168

Tempier, Stephen, 33, 121–23, 135
Theodora (mother of Thomas Aquinas), 19
Tinctor, John, 139
Toledo, Francisco de, 155
Torrell, Jean-Pierre, 185, 192
Tyrrell, George, 179, 181

Urban IV, Pope, 28–29

Valla, Lorenzo, 142
Vann, Gerald, 119
Vazquez, Gabriel, 155
Vio, Tommaso di (Cardinal Cajetan). *See* Cajetan
Vitoria, Francisco de, 147–48

Vivès, Louis, 175
von Balthasar, Hans Urs, 206–07
von Drey, J. S., 165
von Hügel, Friedrich, 179, 181

Walsh, Liam, 115
Weisheipl, James, 192
William de la Mare, 124–25
William of Moerbeke, 29
William of Ockham, 135, 138
William of St. Amour, 26
William of Tocco, 24, 34
Wippel, John, 192
Wittgenstein, Ludwig, 213
Wolff, Christian, 160–61
Writing on the Books of Sentences (Scriptum super libros sententiarum), 23, 41, 68–69, 78, 107, 109, 138, 143

Zigliara, Tommaso, 167, 175

SUBJECT INDEX

abstraction, 46, 94, 172, 194, 200

act and potency, 81, 83, 92, 94, 99, 200

active and contemplative lives, 77, 105–6, 154

acts, human, 45, 50–51, 57, 64, 76–77, 95–102, 111, 130, 132–33, 157, 206

analogy, 10, 57, 88, 92, 119, 128, 145. *See also* language about God

angels, 75, 123, 196

anthropology, 30–31, 33, 42, 46, 53, 62, 75, 77, 93–96, 121, 128, 132, 146–47, 173, 203. *See also* image of God

apophatic theology. *See* theology

apostolic life, 16–17, 26

argument and argumentative, 10, 22, 43, 45–46, 49, 53–54, 56, 60–62, 64–65, 67, 74, 80–82, 87, 108–09, 121, 129, 138–39, 146, 150, 157, 169–70,

201, 203, 212; argument from necessity (*ex necessitate*) and argument from fittingness (*ex convenientia*), 62, 65–66, 71, 77, 108–09

Aristotelian crisis, 30–34

Aristotelianism, 26, 29–33, 35, 41–42, 62, 90, 99, 120–21, 129–30, 145, 194

assumption of human nature by Christ, 77, 110

Augustinianism, 42, 61, 99–101

authority, 8, 12–13, 32, 48, 56, 61–62, 119–20, 141, 149, 157, 159, 169–70, 183, 185, 192; authority, textual (*auctoritas*), 12, 45–46, 53, 65, 67, 80, 108

Averroism, 31–32, 35, 43, 136, 142, 145

baptism, 78, 113–15

beatific vision (*visio beatifica*), 38, 72, 86, 93, 98–101, 111, 200 beatitude (*beatitudo*), 45, 51, 59, 72, 75–76, 86, 93, 96–98, 103, 107, 129, 132–33

being in general (*ens commune*), 43, 63, 82, 84, 87–88, 128, 132, 156, 194, 197; *see also* existence

Bible and Biblical Interpretation, 10–12, 22, 24–25, 35, 37, 41, 46, 49, 53, 58, 60, 62–66, 69–70, 80, 89–90, 93, 100, 108–10, 112, 131, 134, 136–37, 145, 149, 151–52, 178–79, 181–82, 190

body. *See* anthropology

canonization, 24, 36, 40, 119, 134, 184

cause, causality, 3–4, 53, 56, 59–60, 62, 67, 69, 81, 83, 86–87, 91–92, 97, 108, 110, 113–15, 133; instrumental causality, 4, 62, 64, 114–15

change (*motus*), 5, 59, 81, 91–92, 99, 102

charity, virtue of, 37, 61, 76, 102–4, 150

chastity, virtue of, 21, 102

Christ and Christology, 34, 45, 51, 62, 64, 67–73, 77–78, 106–12, 114, 133, 155, 159, 169, 179

church, 7–9, 15, 39, 52, 55, 64–65, 105–07, 112, 134–35, 144, 148–52, 167–68, 171, 182–85, 207–8, 211

Collegio Romano (Gregorian University), 155, 166, 169, 202

commandments, 102, 105

commentary, 2–3, 28–31, 35, 37, 40–41, 46–49, 52, 65–66, 117–18, 134, 136–40, 144–48, 153, 155, 158–61, 170–72, 186–88, 193, 197

conclusions (*conclusiones*), 11, 32, 52, 56, 59–60, 62, 67, 74, 100, 105, 108, 134, 138, 146, 171

confession and confessors, 34, 47, 50, 72, 127, 153, 158

Congregation on the Aids to Grace (*congregatio de auxiliis*), 156–57

connaturality, 4, 60

contemplation, 4–5, 22, 35, 54, 59, 106, 200, 206

contingency, 84, 90

Correctoria literature, 124–26

creation, 5, 44, 70–71, 75, 85, 89–92, 96, 110, 121, 126, 146, 196–97

creature, 5, 60, 68, 75–76, 79, 83, 86–88, 90, 92–95, 127

Councils, general, 10, 38, 149, 169, 171; Trent, Council of, 147, 151–53, 157; Vatican I, Council of, 152, 167, 169; Vatican II, Council of, 166, 180, 184, 191, 207, 212

Counter-Reformation, 153–54

decision, divine, 90–91

demonstration (*demonstratio*), 33, 53, 81, 90

dependence on God, 90–91

desire for God, 86, 93–94, 98

discipline, or learning (*disciplina*), 49, 51–53, 66

disputation (*disputatio*), 14–16, 22, 27, 35–36, 45–47, 49, 155

distinction (*distinctio*), 15, 22, 46, 67, 74, 83, 87, 91–92, 101, 110, 115, 118

doctor, 119, 127, 134, 154, 170, 174, 184; Thomas as Angelic Doctor; (*doctor angelicus*), 140, 154, 165, 175, 183, 185, 211;

doctor *(continued)*
    Thomas as Common Doctor
    (*doctor communis*), 134
doctrine (*doctrina*). *See* sacred
    teaching
Dominican Order and Domini-
    cans, 7, 16–18, 20–21, 27–28,
    31, 33, 36, 39–40, 44, 47,
    50–51, 106, 119–20, 124–27,
    131–32, 135, 139–41, 145, 149,
    152–54, 156–59, 165, 167, 172,
    174–76, 178, 180, 186–92, 209
duration of universe, 33, 35,
    90–91, 121, 126

education, 8–9, 11, 18, 47–51, 108,
    170, 182, 208
emanation and return (*exitus-
    reditus*), 5, 45, 68–71, 74–79,
    89
emotions (*passiones*), 76, 98, 111.
    See also anthropology
end or goal. *See* teleology
Enlightenment, 160–61, 163–64,
    168, 170
epistemology, 93–95, 164,
    172–73, 194, 199, 202–4
equivocation, 88, 119. *See also*
    language about God
eschatology, 45, 107
essence, 82–83, 92, 196–97. *See
    also* being; existence
eternity, 31, 33, 35, 85, 90–91, 121
Eucharist, 29, 39, 78, 113, 115
evil, 42, 75, 86. *See also* sin; vice
existence (*esse*), 82–83, 92, 110,
    126–27, 132, 153, 156, 172,
    196–98, 201–2, 206–7

faith, 10–12, 28, 32–33, 37, 39, 43,
    49–50, 54–55, 61–62, 65, 71,

76, 80, 86, 90, 104, 108–10,
    118, 126, 129–30, 133–34, 138,
    150, 164–65, 170–71, 188–89,
    196, 206, 211; faith seeking
    understanding (*fides quaerens
    intellectum*), 11, 15, 49–50, 52,
    56, 59, 61, 108, 190, 208, 212
fall of humanity, 99–100
Fathers of the church, 10–12, 15,
    29, 34, 112, 141, 154, 161–62,
    170, 188, 191
fideism, 80–81, 208
five ways of proving God's exis-
    tence (*quinque viae*), 79–82
form (and matter), 33, 46, 82–83,
    92, 103, 114, 153, 194
fortitude, virtue of, 104–05
Franciscan Order, 17, 33, 38, 120,
    124–25, 152
freedom and free choice, 71,
    90–91, 96–97, 108, 121, 129,
    156–57, 164, 202–03
friendship, 89, 103–04

gifts of the Holy Spirit, 4–5, 60,
    104–05, 111, 158–59. *See also*
    wisdom
God, general, 44, 46, 52–54, 59,
    62–64, 68–71, 73–75, 79–89,
    103–04, 108, 115, 120, 128, 130,
    142–43, 150, 172, 179, 188, 197,
    200–202, 213; existence as
    God's essence, 63, 82–85, 92,
    196, 201; God's action, 75, 79,
    88–89, 100, 108, 121–22; God's
    goodness, 69–70, 83, 85–88,
    97, 100; God's intellect and
    knowledge, 55, 57, 60, 75, 88,
    91, 95, 132, 156–57, 200; God's
    power, 25, 42, 64, 69, 75;
    God's will and freedom, 62,

75, 83, 88, 91, 101, 129; names
of God, 75, 85; proving God's
existence, 74, 79–82, 132, 159
good and goodness, 53, 63, 75,
84–86, 88, 97–98, 100, 105
grace, 4, 61, 69, 76–77, 86, 93,
96, 98–103, 105, 113–15, 150,
156–58, 195, 202–03, 206;
grace of union in Christ, 110;
operative and cooperative
grace, 101–2, 156–57, 202

habit, 3–4, 58–59, 76, 95–96, 98,
100–101, 105, 111, 128–29, 146
hagiography, 19–40 *passim*, 161.
See also canonization
happiness. *See* beatitude
heaven, 64, 79, 86, 107. *See also*
beatific vision
hell, 79, 107
heresy, 11, 16–17, 50, 61, 108, 131,
143, 149, 157, 179
history of salvation, 46, 64,
69–71, 97, 99, 108–9
Holy Spirit, 101, 114. *See also* gifts
of Holy Spirit
hope, virtue of, 37, 76, 102
Humanism, 137, 140–41, 148
human nature. *See* anthropology

Idealism, 164, 172
image of God (*imago dei*), 69,
93, 95–96, 132–33. *See also*
anthropology
immortality, 31, 34, 107, 114, 142,
145–46
Incarnation of Christ, 28, 45, 62,
77, 97, 99, 106–12, 128. *See also*
Christ and Christology
infallibility, papal, 167, 169–70
infinity, 85, 93, 203

instrument and instrumental
causality. *See* cause, causality
intellect, 31, 35, 43, 46, 85–86,
93–95, 97–98, 111, 123, 128,
131–32, 199–200, 203. *See also*
anthropology

Jesuit Order, 154–59, 161, 165–67,
183–84, 186, 188, 199–206
Jesus Christ. *See* Christ and
Christology
judgment, act of, 3, 27, 39, 58–59,
84, 95, 157, 200–203
justice, virtue of, 104–5
justification, 101, 151–52. *See also*
salvation

knowledge, 6, 15, 24, 46, 49,
53–57, 62–63, 77, 85–87,
94–95, 111, 128, 130, 150, 157,
162, 172, 194–95, 199–206. *See
also* intellect
language about God, 63, 82–88,
108, 128, 132, 213
law, 8, 12–13, 67, 76, 96–97, 99,
147, 210
lectio. See reading
Leonine Edition, x, 175–77, 186
liberal arts, 20
logic, 10–11, 13, 31, 62–63, 67, 82,
86–87, 89, 124, 205
love, 97, 103–4, 112, 130

Master of theology (*magister*),
10, 14–15, 21, 24–25, 27, 31–32,
50, 52, 66, 120–23, 125, 135, 139
Mendicant Orders, 7, 17–18,
25–26, 32, 124. *See also*
Dominican Order; Franciscan
Order
merit, 101, 112

metaphysics, 52–54, 60, 81, 138, 145, 155, 160, 172–73, 180, 183, 192–94, 196–98, 202, 206. *See also* philosophy

Modernism, 178–83, 185, 188

modernity, 164, 166, 168, 178, 187–88, 207

moral theology. *See* theology

motion. *See* change

mysticism, 38, 106, 130, 188, 194–95, 200–201, 204

nature and natural, 53–54, 61, 83, 94, 98–100, 103, 110, 146, 153, 191. *See also* supernatural

necessity. *See* argument

Neo-Augustinianism, 32, 120–21

Neoplatonism, 41–42, 68, 70, 92, 131, 142, 198. *See also* Platonism

New Theology (*la théologie nouvelle*), 184–85, 188, 191

Neothomism. *See* Thomism

Nominalism, 135, 148

One, the, 84–86, 197

ontotheology, 84

operation and cooperation. *See* grace

order and ordering, 3–4, 12, 14–15, 58–59, 66–73, 89, 93, 103, 116, 130, 137, 139, 168, 206

papacy, 7–9, 17–18, 25–26, 28–29, 38–39, 44, 134, 148–49, 151–54, 157–58, 163–71, 174–77, 179–85, 199, 208–11

participation, 31, 35, 72, 92, 94–95, 99, 197–98

Passion of Christ, 78, 108, 112, 114. *See also* Christ and Christology

penance, 17, 78, 107, 113, 115

perfection, 5, 84–88, 98, 106, 109–10, 200

person, notion of, 75, 77, 89, 94, 108, 110, 130

philosophy, 2, 13–14, 27–28, 33, 42–43, 52–55, 61–63, 69–70, 80–81, 84, 90, 93, 98, 118–19, 121–24, 127–36, 138–39, 142–44, 148, 159–60, 163–65, 168–72, 176–85, 187, 189, 192–200, 202, 204–5, 211–13; Christian philosophy, 193, 195–97, 211

Platonism, 41–42, 92, 94, 141–43, 198. *See also* Neoplatonism

potency. *See* act and potency

poverty. *See* apostolic life

prayer, 23, 194

preaching, 14–18, 20, 27, 50, 72, 131, 142

predestination, 156–57

predication. *See* logic

principle, 13–14, 46, 49, 56, 58–60, 62, 67, 70, 81, 98, 105, 108–9, 118, 124, 127, 134, 137–38, 171, 183, 207

printing, 137, 143–44, 146, 154, 175–77

procession (*processio*), 68, 75, 89. *See also* emanation and return

proof and proving. *See* argument

Protestantism. *See* Reformation

providence, 39, 75, 90, 156

prudence, virtue of, 104–5

question (*quaestio*), 12–13, 24, 27, 41–42, 44–45, 48–50, 67, 109, 137, 155 reading (*lectio*), 12, 15, 41

reason, 4, 12, 28, 32–33, 35,
54–55, 60–61, 80, 86, 89,
90–93, 105, 118, 126, 129,
133–34, 145, 160, 163–65,
170–71, 196, 211–12

redemption. *See* salvation

Reformation, 140, 148–51

relation (*relatio*), 75, 87, 89,
91, 133

relics, 34, 39–40

Renaissance, 140–43, 190

resurrection of the body, 72, 107

Resurrection of Jesus, 78, 111–12

revelation, 4, 28, 32–33, 55–56,
59, 60–62, 71, 88, 92, 99,
128–29, 133–34, 185, 194, 196.
See also faith

sacrament, 29, 43, 45, 51, 71, 78,
107, 112–15, 151–52, 159

sacred teaching (*sacra doctrina*),
3–4, 46, 51–73 *passim*, 79, 85,
89, 93, 108, 128, 130, 138, 142,
146, 159–60. *See also* teaching

Salamanca School (*Salmanticenses*), 159–60

salvation, 5, 46, 53–55, 66, 72,
100–02, 107–08, 112, 114, 129,
150, 156, 159, 210

sanctification, 113–14

sapientia. *See* wisdom

satisfaction, 112

Scholasticism, 7, 9–16, 55, 111,
116, 120–22, 135, 141–44,
148, 151, 170, 177, 181–83, 185,
188, 190–91, 195; Baroque
Scholasticism, 153, 190–91;
Neoscholasticism, 41, 167, 169,
177–78, 180–81, 207; Protestant Scholasticism, 151

science (*scientia*), 4, 49, 52, 54,
56–60, 64, 66, 71, 121, 129–30,
138, 194–95, 200

Scotism, 127, 135, 152, 155–56

seminary, 158, 160, 173–74,
180–81, 183–84

sign, 15, 113–15

simpleness (*simplicitas*), 82–86.
See also God

sin, 50–51, 109–10, 112, 128, 148,
150–51

soul, nature and powers of. *See*
anthropology

substance and substantial form,
33, 84, 110, 123, 197. *See also*
form

supernatural, the, 5, 53–54, 93,
98–100, 129, 191, 194

synthesis, 7, 28, 37, 40–41,
43–44, 58, 69, 89, 107, 113, 130,
201, 203

teaching, 6, 10, 13–15, 24, 31,
35–36, 40, 48–52, 55, 58,
65–66, 108, 129, 133–35, 137,
139–40, 144–45, 147, 149–50,
158, 165–66, 168–70, 173, 178,
183, 187, 195, 208. *See also*
sacred teaching

teleology, 53, 59, 72–73, 93–94,
96–98, 105, 129, 133, 146

temperance, virtue of, 104–5

textbooks, 11–15, 31, 48, 50, 63,
120, 126, 135, 139, 144, 160–61,
174, 183

theology, general, 9–10, 27–28,
30–32, 44, 49–50, 52, 55,
72, 106, 118–19, 121–25,
127–34, 147, 149–50, 152, 161,
163–65, 168–73, 178, 183–85,
188–92, 197, 204–6, 211–12;

theology *(continued)*
apophatic theology, 48, 63, 79, 82, 84–87, 89, 128, 131, 133–36, 143–44, 167; doctrinal theology, 37, 54, 65–66, 206; historical theology, 161, 169, 172–73, 189; moral theology, 50–51, 64, 72, 96–97, 105, 120, 127; philosophical theology, 54, 80, 212

Thomism: general, 82, Chapters 4–5 *passim*, 211, 213–14; Analytical Thomism, 213; Byzantine Thomism, 135–36; Chinese Thomism, 155; First Thomism, 125–27; Jewish Thomism, 136; Metaphysical Thomism, 187, 192–98; Monumental Thomism, 173, 184–85; Neothomism, 118, Chapter 5 *passim*, 210; Revived Thomism, 187–92; Second Thomism, 144, 147, 172; Strict-Observance Thomism, 187–88, 191, 196, 213; Suarezian Thomism, 156, 166, 183; Transcendental Thomism, 187, 198–206; Twenty-Four-Thesis Thomism, 183–84

transcendence of God, 63, 85–90

Trent, Council of. *See* Councils

Trinity, 28, 54, 61, 75–79, 88–89, 130, 133, 203, 205

truth, 13, 26, 28, 33, 42, 46, 54, 58–61, 64–65, 72, 80, 82, 88–89, 93–94, 108, 133–34, 149, 152, 160, 165, 167, 171, 179–80, 189, 199, 207, 211

unicity of form, 33–34, 121, 123–24, 126. *See also* form and matter

union, 98, 100; hypostatic union of Christ, 77–78, 107–10

university, 7, 9–16, 18, 20, 25–26, 160–61, 171, 177–78

univocity, 87–88, 128. *See also* language about God

Vatican Councils. *See* Councils

vice, 50, 72–73, 76, 96, 102, 104–5. *See also* evil; sin

virtue, general, 3, 36, 42, 50, 72–73, 76, 96, 102, 105, 114; cardinal virtues, 77, 102, 104–5; theological virtues, 37, 76, 102

war, 104, 147

will, 61–62, 93–93, 97–98, 101–03, 128. *See also* anthropology

wisdom (*sapientia*), 3–6, 25, 28, 56–61, 63, 68, 71, 85–87, 104, 116, 150, 170–71, 194, 214

Word of God, 45, 60, 107, 109–10, 114, 128, 132. *See also* Christ and Christology